The Sea-Side Book
Being An Introduction To
The Natural History Of The
British Coasts

William H. Harvey

Alpha Editions

This Edition Published in 2021

ISBN: 9789354542824

Design and Setting By
Alpha Editions
www.alphaedis.com
Email – info@alphaedis.com

As per information held with us this book is in Public Domain.
This book is a reproduction of an important historical work. Alpha Editions
uses the best technology to reproduce historical work in the same manner
it was first published to preserve its original nature. Any marks or number
seen are left intentionally to preserve its true form.

THE SEA-SIDE BOOK;

BEING

AN INTRODUCTION TO
THE NATURAL HISTORY OF THE BRITISH COASTS.

BY

W. H. HARVEY, M.D., M.R.I.A.,

KEEPER OF THE HERBARIUM OF THE UNIVERSITY OF DUBLIN, AND
PROFESSOR OF BOTANY TO THE ROYAL DUBLIN SOCIETY

"LONDON BRIDGE" ROCK AT TORQUAY.

NEW EDITION.

LONDON:
JOHN VAN VOORST, PATERNOSTER ROW.

M.DCCC.XLIX.

TO

JOHN TODHUNTER, Jun.,

OF DUBLIN,

This Little Book is dedicated

BY

HIS AFFECTIONATE UNCLE,

THE AUTHOR.

LIST OF ILLUSTRATIONS.

"London Bridge" Rock at Torquay	On Title Page.
Oratory of S. Piran in the Sands	1
Shrimp and Prawn Catchers	21
Dunlin Sandpipers	23
Egg of Shark	31
Buccinum undatum and Nest	32
Purpura Lapillus and Eggs	33
Natica monilifera	33
Flustra foliacea	44
Alcyonium digitatum	47
Tor-Abbey Rocks and Headland, with Berry-Head in the distance	52
Root of Laminaria	58
Ulva crispa	60
Codium tomentosum	60
Bryopsis plumosa	61
Cladophora Hutchinsiæ	62
Lichina pygmæa and Confinis	68
Padina pavonia	70
Griffithsia corallina	72
Polysiphoniæ parasitica	73
Corallina officinalis	76
Actinia bellis	78
Actiniæ, or Sea Anemones	79
Egg of Sponge	83
Coryne pusilla and magnified portion	87
Sertularia filicula and magnified portion	89
Plumularia cristata and magnified vesicle	90
Caryophyllea Smithii	93
Lucernaria auricula	94
Various Species of Lepraliæ, magnified	96
Appendage of Cellularia	97
Botryllus	99
Shell from Lycia, E. F.	103
Pholas candida	104
Limpet's Tongue	107
Ancula cristata	108
Chiton marginatus and fascicularis	109
Nassa reticulata	112
Dredging	116

viii   LIST OF ILLUSTRATIONS.

NATURALIST'S DREDGE	Page 117
DRAG	119
NULLIPORES	121
PLANARIA VITTATA	123
SERPULA	128
PENTACRINUS EUROPEUS	134
PEDICELLARIÆ	144
THYONE PAPILLOSA	149
VIRGULARIA MIRABILIS	152
ZOEA OF THE CRAB	165
ICEBERG, WITH SEASCAPE	168
ISTHMIA OBLIQUATA	171
LICMOPHORA FLABELLATA	172
LAGENÆ	180
ROTALIA BECCARII AND POLYSTOMELLA CRISPA	181
BEROE	189
VELELLA	191
MEDUSÆ BUDS IN VARIOUS STAGES	195
YOUNG OF MEDUSÆ FORMING	197
SALPA RUNCINATA, IN ITS FREE AND ASSOCIATED STATES	199
SEA BIRDS	203
HORNED POPPY	205
SALICORNIA HERBACEA	208
GLAUX MARITIMA	209
STORM PETREL	231
PENTELASMIS ANATIFERA	232
YOUNG CIRRHIPODE, MAGNIFIED	234
LIMNORIA TEREBRANS	237
CHELURA TEREBRANS	237
MARINE GRAPES	239

For a more detailed History of the Subjects comprised in this Volume the Reader is referred to the following Works:—

MR. YARRELL'S *History of British Birds, and his History of British Fishes.*—PROFESSOR BELL'S *History of British Crustacea.*—PROFESSOR EDWARD FORBES *History of British Starfishes, &c.*—PROFESSOR E. FORBES AND MR. HANLEY'S *British Mollusca.*—DR. JOHNSTON'S *History of British Zoophytes, and his History of British Sponges, &c.*—MESSRS. ALDER AND HANCOCK'S *Nudibranchiate Mollusca.* — PROFESSOR HARVEY'S *Phycologia Britannica, or his Manual of British Marine Algæ.*—PROFESSOR ANSTED'S *Geology.*—PROFESSOR RYMER JONES' *General Outline of the Animal Kingdom, and the First Volume of his Natural History of Animals.*—SIR JOHN G. DALYELL'S *Rare and Remarkable Animals of Scotland.*

ORATORY OF ST. PIRAN IN THE SANDS.

See page 10.

CHAPTER I.

INTRODUCTORY.

It is scarcely more than a century since the several sciences to which we apply the general name of Natural History, began to rouse themselves from a sleep into which they had fallen nearly two thousand years before. The middle ages of Natural History are peculiarly the dark ages, and the darkness was dense as it was long. Throughout this long period observers were scarce; theorisers and commentators, critics of subjects which they could not comprehend, were numerous; and the body of naturalists occupied themselves in specious dreams. Here and there, like the flashes which cheer the darkness of the polar winter, noble minds rose above their fellows to declare the truths which they had observed or discovered; but such lights were rare, and soon put aside—they could not be extinguished—by the race over which a busy dulness reigned supreme.

The writers of the middle ages had built up in their own minds a perfect system, as it was supposed; and this they imagined to be the system of the universe. Instead, therefore, of seeking out, by patient observation, the facts of Nature, and reasoning upon them, they employed themselves in cutting down to their own notions of propriety every fact which seemed to contradict what the schoolmen considered a law of Nature. A glaring instance of such prejudiced explanation is found in the theories gravely put forward by learned men to explain the existence of organic fossils. Marine petrifactions—fishes, shells, corals—were found imbedded in rocks, or in the soil, in places far removed from the existing sea, and at a considerable height above its level,—in the upland country, and even on the tops of mountains. The wise men of those days (so late as the year 1680) explained the phenomena by supposing a "plastic power" in Nature, which was exerted in moulding the living rock into mimic representations of animals and plants, for no better purpose, seemingly, than to puzzle and amuse the vulgar. This was cutting the knot of difficulty after a strange fashion. It was contrary to their theory to believe that the sea had ever occupied the places in which the marine productions were found. If it had not, how could these have got there? There was no reply but the resolute denial that the fossils were really the relics of marine creatures; and this, in spite of the evidence of their senses, or the deductions of sound reason, these pseudo-philosophers unblushingly asserted. It was thus that the facts of Nature were habitually twisted to suit the requirings of a preconceived theory; and thus laborious lives were spent to no other purpose than in heaping up a mass of unreadable nonsense in our libraries.

The enunciation of the inductive philosophy was the first great blow to the fame of these writers. The perfect system of the universe was found to be no longer tenable; it fell almost at the first onset, and with it fell the charm which had embalmed every opinion handed down from classic times. The Book of Nature began to be studied with ardour, and in a new and unfettered spirit. No longer clogged with theories, naturalists found that, so far from its having been exhausted by the labours of their predecessors, Natural History was full, to overflowing, of novel interest. Facts were no longer tried by traditional authority; but tradition was subjected to the close inquisition of newly-observed facts. In every country observers were at work; and, instead of the somnambulism of the preceding ages, naturalists, like men newly risen, went forth in their morning strength and ardour to the labour of the day. The fair sun of science was already above the horizon, and it was their privilege to drink in his earliest beams.

So long as Natural History was encumbered with its pseudo-classical incubus its votaries were few in number. The more it grew into a science founded on observation, the more it attracted popular attention. The writings of LINNÆUS, composed in a clear and elegant style, and offering a systematic arrangement such as all could readily understand, contributed more than those of any other naturalist to the spread of a taste for his favourite science. He was eminently a popular writer, and, no matter what criticism may now be passed on his system, it must be admitted that to it is greatly owing the rapidity with which the natural sciences advanced in public favour in the early part of last century. Had his followers possessed a tithe of his comprehensive and singularly-penetrating mind, they would have saved his memory from many an undeserved reproach. No man ever had a truer eye for a natural group, or was more deeply impressed with the value of a natural system. He has indeed left us, in his Genera, especially of *Insects* and *Shells*, grand outlines of such a system, sketched by a master's hand. But he felt that the time for erecting the temple of Nature had not come, and that his own province lay in preparing materials for the building, and to this task he devoted the chief energies of his mind.

We of the present generation are, perhaps, too apt to think that sufficient materials have already been amassed, and to set ourselves—often with but a very superficial knowledge of even a single department of a single science—to work out a system which shall embrace a much wider field, perhaps one that shall attempt to be a System of Nature. Hence the numerous systems, all called "natural," which have been proposed, both in Zoology and Botany, within the last fifty years. Hence, too, the still stranger systems and anti-systems which the history of Geology exhibits, where the same fact

THEORIES.

is often adduced by different writers as the most convincing proof in favour of directly opposite views of the history of the world. These discrepancies are sufficient to prove to any unprejudiced mind that the requisite materials for constructing a perfectly natural system are not yet accumulated, and that in every department of Natural History patient observers are still required, who will be contented to store up facts, and to work out such parts of a general system as they find to be within their legitimate reach, abstaining from all general views that are not warranted by the amount, either of their own knowledge, or of that of the scientific world in general. Bold minds will now and then run a-head of absolute discoveries, and by lucky anticipation will sometimes point in the right direction. Deeply informed and comprehensive intellects will discover glimpses through the haze, like the looming of distant land, where common observers can see no indications of a solution, and their "guesses at truth," being built partly on real induction, partly on skilfully-applied analogies, often open up to us correct views of the order of Nature which subsequent discoveries only confirm and strengthen. Such minds will ever be cautious in advancing theories : but how many hasty observers, admiring the brilliant results attained by the skilful "guesser," ignorant of the liabilities to error, and therefore despising caution, rush forward on their course, and propose to the world their fanciful schemes as important discoveries. In the republic of science there is no longer a recognized head. Each panter after fame may set up a system of his own. There is no controlling power but the slow-working verdict of the general voice. That, indeed, operates surely and calmly, like the inexorable laws of Nature, and consigns each bubble theory, in due time, to merited forgetfulness : but this operation may be a long one, and many a theoriser, for the false excitement of temporary notoriety, will risk the possession of enduring fame.

The present age has produced many of these pseudo-naturalists, though not so many as that immediately preceding it. The spirit is not extinct : and therefore it is that I would caution my younger fellow-students, for whom these pages are written, against allowing their imaginations to be carried away by specious theories, or any theories which do not proceed from a deep study of Nature. Much more would I caution them against building systems of their own. Their place clearly is, to learn and not to teach, and until they have brought together a very considerable amount of observations they can scarcely have an adequate conception of what a system should be. In heaping together these observations, they will find real pleasure, and will become, as they proceed, more and more sensible of the capacity of mind and knowledge which is required in him who shall venture to sketch out a "*Systema Naturæ*." Let no man boast, like the irreverent monument to Buffon, of having " a mind equal to the majesty of Nature ;"—and let none of us act as if we laid claim to such a mind. The portion of the created universe with which the naturalist occupies himself is indeed small, if we compare our world with the stellar system, and estimate its value by the line and the plummet ; but, the more we become conversant with its heights and depths, the more shall we find that size and weight ought to have no place in our estimation of the great or the little in Nature: for they appear to have no place in the mind of the Author of Nature. The same skill and care are employed in the formation and adaptation of the minutest animal or plant as in that of the largest; and the same law that governs the formation of a rain-drop, influences not merely that of our own world, but extends throughout the immeasurable regions of space. In Nature everything displays the same evidence of greatness of design, sufficient, when duly appreciated, to fill the largest intellect to overflowing, and to make it sensible that so far from having a capacity " equal to the majesty" of what it contemplates, its utmost stretchings are insufficient to comprehend the fulness of a single natural law.

In contrast to the inventors of fanciful systems, how gladly do we turn to such a writer as Gilbert White, the well-known author of " The Natural History of Selborne." Within the bounds of a single country parish he found ample materials for one of the most delightful and instructive books of Natural History ever written. It does not require to be located in a peculiarly favoured district to discover sufficient to arrest the attention of the observant naturalist, or even to add something to the general stock of knowledge. The naturalist is more independent of circumstances than most men. Give him fields and hedges, the barren moor, or the quarry,— from each and all he will collect a store of useful and entertaining facts. No part of the country is so absolutely barren that it will not afford employment to the cultivator of some department of Natural History : and employment of that nature that will keep his mind pleasantly and profitably occupied, in the midst of the most complete retirement. One therefore wonders that a taste for Natural History is not the universal accompaniment of a country life.

But if country life naturally lead us to contemplate the objects of creation with which we are there surrounded, how much more does a residence, and especially an occasional residence, on the sea-coast attract us into the field of observation. The numerous marine watering-places, which are thronged in the summer and autumn months, ought to be so many schools for naturalists. Placed on all our coasts, they offer the greatest variety of aspect and climate that the limited shores of the British Islands can supply. The sheltered bay — the open strand—the bold rocky barrier against which breakers constantly roll—each has its peculiar animal and vegetable inhabitant; and each variety of shore is more or less perfectly represented in one or other of our watering-places. By visiting different parts, therefore, of the coast in succession, year by year, we may investigate to the greatest advantage the productions of the sea. These are never exhausted: and once that an interest in the pursuit is awakened, it never flags. There is no need to import the winter resources of cities—balls, parties, and theatrical representations — to the watering-place. Half the year ought to suffice for these amusements. Let the summer and the sea-side preserve their native pleasures undisturbed. There is so much to be enjoyed on the sea-shore when the mind is once opened to the pleasure afforded by the study of Natural History, that no other stimulus is wanted to keep the interest of the visitor constantly awake. Instead of finding his time hang heavily, he will often wonder how rapidly the long summer-day has flown by, while he has been occupied with some investigation in the midst of which darkness overtakes him. When visiting the sea, to seek relaxation from business, it is astonishing with what zest a person will enter on the pursuit of Natural History, and how invigorating and refreshing he will find it. After a short time, the mind of an habitually busy man finds no relief in complete idleness. He must occupy himself in some manner. He is removed from his ordinary business—perhaps, forbidden by a physician from receiving letters that require thought; his mind is too active to rest unemployed, and there is nothing in the neighbourhood to rouse him. If on the sea-shore, and happily possessing a turn for Natural History, he is at once supplied with occupation of the most healthful character. His pursuits lead him to take exercise of body, and, without fatiguing the mind, give it that pleasurable excitement which rapidly restores its tone when suffering from having been over-wrought. It matters little to which of the Natural History sciences he devotes his attention, or whether each in turn engages it. Probably, a valetudinarian will find most relief in variety. He can indulge a taste for Geology either in investigating the sections of strata which the headlands of the coast often admirably exhibit, or in watching the thousand evidences of forces in operation which are gradually changing the level of our present seas, and which explain to us the greater operations of a former era, or show us how, in slowly accumulating periods, changes as great are in preparation even now. The formation of beds of the remains of recent testacea, crustacea, and fishes; the gradual induration of conglomerates under the sea; and the drifting of sands by the wind, may all be observed in different parts of our coast, and in some to a very remarkable degree. The changes effected by wind-blown sands have very materially altered the features of several parts of the British coasts, converting tracts of fertile land into deserts as sterile as those of Africa. Lyell mentions a district in the north of Cornwall, once cultivated and inhabited, where the drifted sands now form hills composed of minute fragments of sea-shells, several hundred feet above the level of the sea. Here the sand may in several places be found undergoing a process of induration, and in some parts the change is so far advanced that blocks are used as building-stone; and thus the geologist can trace the gradual formation of a sandstone-rock. But the interest of this locality is not confined to the geologist. The archæologist will visit it as the residence of one of the early missionaries, by whose labours Christianity was introduced into this remote part of Britain, and where, on the overthrow of so many British churches by the subsequent incursions of an unchristian horde, the light of truth continued to shine till the commencement of a happier era. Here, toward the close of the fourth century, St. Piran, " born of noble parents, in the county of Ossory, in Ireland, A.D. 352, and converted to the Christian faith in 382, having been ordained bishop at Rome, fixed his abode among a simple people, and passed a long and exemplary life in instructing them. Nor did he confine himself to the functions of his sacred calling, but, we are told, he was equally zealous in instructing his parishioners in the useful arts, and especially in the working of metals. Hence, it is not without reason that " the Cornish miners venerate the name of Piranus as their tutelary saint and benefactor; and to this day the tinners of Cornwall keep his feast on the 5th of March, and hold a fair near his church in honour of St. Piranus." The church, long buried under the sands, has recently been exhumed, and the vignette at the head of this chapter represents its present state.* Another instance occurs on the coast of Suffolk, where, in the lapse of a century, the sands have spread over more than 1000 acres of land. On the coast of Sligo an equally destructive sand-inundation has taken place, and, though partially checked, is still in progress. This has already destroyed from seven to eight hundred acres of fertile land, burying in its course a considerable village. Strange to say, the village is not yet a " Deserted Village," though buried in the midst of a desert. Its inhabitants still cling to their wretched huts, only the roofs of which now rise above the sands, and these, with the entrances, are kept clear only by the constant labours of the inmates. It is a singular sight in walking over extensive sandy downs, where

* See an interesting publication by the Rev. Collins Trelawny, called " Perranzabuloe—the lost church found," 1836, and also " Perranzabuloe; with an Account of the Past and Present State of the Oratory of St. Piran in the Sands," by the Rev. W. Haslam, 1844.

scarcely a blade is seen, to come suddenly on a rude chimney from which the peat-smoke rises, and to see a pig, followed by a troop of ragged children, rise up from under our feet. Much care has been taken to induce the occupants of these tenements, who subsist on fishing, to quit the ground, but hitherto unsuccessfully. They pay no rent for the burrows; and are contented to act as geological hour-glasses.

In exploring maritime scenes like this, the geologist, not to speak of the philanthropist, will find interesting objects of research. If he be a botanist, he will probably occupy himself also in devising plans for the detention of the sands, and their gradual fixation and conversion into cultivable soil. It is well known that many plants may be advantageously used as binders to loose sands. Of these, the Sand-reed (*Ammophila arundinacea*), which naturally grows on the sandy shores of Europe, is one of the best. Its roots penetrate to a considerable depth, ramifying in all directions, and forming a complete system of rope-work which soon binds together the loosest sands: while its strong tall leaves protect the surface of the soil from drought, and afford shelter to numerous small plants, which soon grow between the reeds, and gradually form a new green surface on the bed of sand. Were this reed planted on the Sligo sands, and protected for a very few years from the donkeys of the imbedded inhabitants, the further progress of the sand-flood would be effectually stopped, and the land now lost to cultivation gradually restored to a part, at least, of its former value. Several other plants will flourish under the protection of the Sand-reed. One of the most valuable (recommended a few years ago by Mr. W. Andrews *) is the Sea-pea (*Lathyrus maritimus*), which produces a fair crop of excellent herbage, while its penetrating roots bind the sands nearly equally with those of the Sand-reed. Were the latter planted on the most exposed places, and the *Lathyrus* under its lee, a most valuable herbage would be acquired. The *Lathyrus* is perennial; if browsed by cattle it does not often blossom, but it extends, by means of runners and suckers, over a wide space, forming a close carpet of nourishing leaves.

Inquiries such as these are, however, more the *applications* of Botany. I would rather speak of the science, apart from its economic relations, as of itself affording enjoyment to the invalid who visits the shore in search of health and strength. When land plants cease to attract his attention, the sea has vegetable treasures in great variety and of inconceivable beauty. The number of British sea-weeds, of the larger class, is not far from four hundred, and if we add purely microscopic species, we shall have upwards of five hundred kinds. In collecting and preparing specimens of these beautiful objects, and tracing out the affinities which link one kind with another, and bring the whole into a well-ordered family, many happy hours may be filled up. Nor is this a selfish pleasure. The true naturalist is always ready to share his pleasures with others, and only half enjoys what he cannot share. The value he attaches to the acquisition of a new plant is quite different from that by which a mere collector estimates his treasure. A collector seeks for unique specimens,

* In a paper read before the Dublin Natural History Society.

and will even destroy duplicates, that he may enjoy the silly boast of having the only specimen in existence. A naturalist ever wishes for a series, that he may trace the connexion between one form and another, and thus see the limit of variation in different species and genera. He works with a constant remembrance of the unity of Nature. The more he discovers traces of affinity between different groups, the more the unity of design manifests itself; and the more his conceptions of a personality in the scheme of Nature are strengthened, and become fixed. From faint and weak beginnings, they gradually expand, and acquire the solidity of truth. Thus, step by step, and as it were "from glory to glory," the mind of the true naturalist is led on to the discovery of laws, and to a just appreciation of the System of Nature.

Pleasures of this kind do not belong to any one department of Natural History in particular. I have alluded to them under the head of Botany; but, in truth, Zoology, in its far greater copiousness and variety, offers an immeasurably wider field. The sea teems with animal life. The various classes of marine animals, and the innumerable species comprised in the whole, are full of interest. Few, even of the most careless, can visit the shore without being struck by their beauty. The gathering of shells is a favourite amusement; but few know anything of the curious animals which have dwelt in them. The dead husks of Zoophytes attract us by their gracefulness and by the truth with which they simulate a vegetable form; but of the animals whose habitations they are, most persons are ignorant of the very existence, believing that the horny skeleton is a veritable sea-weed. The very Jelly-fish, as it swims in the wave, expanding and contracting its umbrella, and thus propelling itself through the water, has its beauty ; but few are aware of the singularity of its history,—how its eggs are of the nature of seeds, which, sown on their rocky bed, sprout and grow, throwing out buds and suckers, each of which forms an animal stem, quite unlike the parent Jelly-fish ; till, at a certain time, young Jelly-fish begin to be formed, and to be thrown off by the several branches, just as flowers are formed, and expand on the several branches that originate from a vegetable-seed. And if the abject Jelly-fish, whose body consists of little more than organized water, have a history so wonderful, shall we not expect to find, in tracing the history of other tribes of animals, matter of equal interest ? The structures, as we ascend in the scale, gradually become more complex ; and if those strange metamorphoses which arrest our attention in the lowest tribes give place to more accustomed phenomena, we are amply compensated by the progressive developement of the wonderful faculty of instinct. In observing the variations of structure of the analogous organs of different animals, and noticing how, according to the necessities of their life, they are provided with proper instruments, innumerable proofs of the care of Providence over His creatures are offered to our contemplation. These cannot fail to interest us, if for no other reason, because they forcibly remind us of our own dependence on the same bountiful Hand, and thus soothe the most desponding with the thought that, if creatures so humble in the scale of creation are cared for, and their wants supplied, the human soul, though linked to a frail body, and placed in a world that seems as nothing in the universe, must, in the sight of its Author, be of that inestimable worth attributed to it by Revelation. If the truths of Astronomy witness to the majesty of God, those of Natural History witness no less to the proper dignity of man; and while the first teach us to humble ourselves before Him "who inhabiteth eternity," the second show us that true humility consists, not in supposing ourselves to be beneath the care, or unworthy the notice, of the "High and Lofty One," but in claiming the privileges of that position in His creation which He has assigned to us, and fulfilling its duties because they are of His requiring.

Such, then, are some of the pleasures of Natural History, whatever branch of the subject we select for our researches. I have glanced at those pleasures under the heads Geology, Botany, and Zoology. Each of these might be again divided; and the last, especially, is so extensive that its several branches are spoken of as distinct sciences. Thus we have Ornithology, Ichthyology, Entomology, Conchology, &c., all branches of the great science of Zoology. The British amateur-naturalist is particularly fortunate in possessing a series of admirable monographs, copiously illustrated by figures, on each of the several zoological sciences; so that, whatever tribe he wishes to study, he can have the advantage of consulting a carefully written, systematic work, which places that particular tribe distinctly before him, and gives him all the striking points of the history of the animals composing it, so far as they are known to naturalists. Yarrell's Histories of British Birds and Fishes : Forbes's Star-fishes; Bell's Crustacea, and Johnston's Zoöphytes, need no commendation. And when the whole series is completed, by the History of British Shells (just commenced), and the splendid work on the Naked-gilled Mollusca publishing under the auspices of the Ray Society, the Zoology of Great Britain will be more perfectly illustrated than that of any other country. In other countries the student has either to consult a general Zoology, or at best a *Fauna* of the country, comprising an account —necessarily brief and imperfect—of all its animals. How few single authors are capable of writing equally well on every tribe, included in a general *Fauna*, if the country whose animals are described be extensive. Some one tribe has engaged more of the author's attention than another, and an undue prominence will thence be given to his favourite. But where each author selects his own tribe, and devotes his whole attention to it, we have in the combined work of several pens the most perfect of general Zoologies. This is precisely what we shall possess in Great Britain when the series of monographs to which I have alluded is finished.

To render these monographs as perfect as possible is the interest of every student of Natural History; and the humblest worker in the field, if careful to see with his own eyes, and record faithfully what he sees, can materially assist the labours of the author. A single, unassisted individual would require the eyes of an Argus, and the hands and heads of a Briareus, to bring together the mass of facts and observations contained in one of these monographs. Such works presuppose the examination of every part of our coasts at all seasons of the year. It falls to no man's lot to make such extensive investigations. But the results of the common labours of many individuals scattered along the shore, concentrated in the author's study, accomplish the work far more rapidly and more perfectly than could possibly be done by any other means. Notwithstanding all that has been done of late years the subject is yet very far from being exhausted. New species and even new genera, are still continually met with among both marine plants and animals on the British coasts; and this, not merely among the more minute and obscure kinds, where such occurrences constantly take place, but among the larger and more perfectly organised classes. The pleasure of adding a new member, never before noticed by man, to the list of known beings must, perhaps, be felt before it can be understood. We experience, in some measure, a parental fondness for an object which we have been the first to bring to light: and with this often mixes a good slice of self-complacency at our own wonderful acuteness. This last feeling is often very silly, for, probably, it was good luck more than sagacity which threw the object in our way: and any one else of common observation, might have acted his part as well. It is something to have worked out a difficult problem requiring mental exertion; or to have been the first to distinguish accurately between two different animals or plants which were before wrongly confounded together; but to plume oneself on having picked up, for the first time, a shell or a sea-weed, which any one visiting the same ground might have equally done, is simply childish.

I speak now of that improper egotism which takes almost as much credit to itself as if it were the *author* of what it has found. I am very far from condemning the pure-minded joy, one of the most delightful feelings of a naturalist, which springs freely in his heart, and glistens in his eye, when first it rests upon an unknown object. This feeling is a mixture of warm affections which cannot confine themselves to a single breast, but instantly seek for sympathy. The first impulse is, to exhibit the novelty to another that he may share our delight, and that we may see him do so. And if there be none to sympathise, how naturally the grateful heart looks up and worships the Author of its enjoyment! Cold as the heart's feelings may be at other times, the fervour of the moment awakens all its better nature. This enjoyment may seem a small thing to call forth gratitude, when we are accustomed to receive so many blessings at the hand of God in a thankless or indifferent spirit. These blessings we seem to look on as our birthright, as members of His family; but the discovery of a new object among the works of creation acts like a special revelation, however small, to ourselves as individuals, and this feeling of individuality touches a chord in the human breast which is ever ready to vibrate. The man whose life is saved by what appears to be a special interference of Providence in his favour, feels strongly what all ought to feel who know that at every moment of our lives the same care is exercised upon us. But the care in the one case is for the general good, the interest of which often calls for individual suffering; in the other, the welfare of the individual seems the special object of providential forethought. The latter brings God as it were personally before us. He is no longer merely the Creator exercising oversight over a vast dominion, but he is our Preserver, protecting us in our going forth and coming in. Similar, though weaker, are the feelings called forth by a closer insight into Nature, and a more intimate acquaintance with her works. When we begin the study, our conception of the Author of Nature may be diffuse—a vague idea as of some illimitable Power, in ceaseless action; but the more we pursue this delightful study, the more we recognise, if we work in a proper spirit, proofs of the *personality* of God. Though now we can know Him but in part, and only see Him reflected in his works as it were " through a glass darkly," we look forward to a time when we shall behold Him "face to face," and shall know Him, " even as we ourselves are known."

SHRIMPERS OF THE ENGLISH COAST.

CHAPTER II.

THE SANDS AND THEIR PRODUCTIONS.

LARGE tracts of sand, exposed to the atmosphere, are proverbially monotonous and desert. Their surface is too loose and uncertain, and water finds its way through them with too great facility, to admit of the growth of a varied vegetation or to afford food and shelter to many animal inhabitants. In a great measure, this barren character applies to extensive sand deposits under the sea; and yet the sandy sea-shore has many attractions which the sandy land-down cannot boast of. The constant flow of the ocean binds together the unsettled particles of sand, and the retreat of the tide from such a coast, if it afford the visitor no other enjoyment, gives him a delightfully smooth and firm promenade, generally of considerable length and breadth; while it rarely happens that monotony is so absolute as to destroy the picturesque associations of the shore. The constant pulsation of the waves on the margin of the tide, far from affecting us with the sense of monotony, serves rather to soothe the mind; while the changes of light and shade on the surface of the sea supply sufficient variety to keep the senses awake. And these changes are quite sufficient, even on the tamest shores, to arrest the attention. Few have attempted to paint coast scenes like those which Crabbe so graphically brings before us :—

> " Where all beside is pebbly length of shore,
> And far as eye can reach, it can discern no more; "

and none with his power of description. The coast which awakened his genius is one of the least picturesque in England; but he saw it with the eyes of a poet and a naturalist. And all who learn the use of similar organs of vision will find that there is no place so dull as not to afford us abundant sources of pleasure.

If we do nothing but watch the flocks of sea-birds which, on the recess of the tide, are attracted to the shore in search of food, their habits will soon begin to interest us. Gulls, Terns, and Sandpipers, of various species, will then become familiar friends; and in watching their various ways, and tracing them when they leave us,—discovering whence they come, and to what country they annually migrate, we shall begin to feel a strong interest in all that concerns them. The Dunlin, the most common of the Sandpipers (*Tringa variabilis*) is found all round our coasts, where it collects, on sandy shores, in vast flocks, which, on the recess of every tide, are busily occupied in searching along the margin of the sea for the minute marine animals, on which they feed. In summer, this active little bird

DUNLIN SANDPIPERS.

deserts its marine haunts, and retires to moors and unfrequented places, similar to those selected by the Plover, where it makes its simple nest and rears its brood. In August, both the young and the old birds return to the coast, and it is then especially that the most numerous and most active flocks are to be seen. Yarrell * well describes them as "incessantly upon the move, shifting their ground perpetually, running nimbly along, or taking short flights from place to place, frequently wading to follow the aquatic insects, worms, mollusca,

* Brit. Birds, iii. p. 82.

and the smaller thin-skinned crustacea, which are put in motion by every receding wave. If disturbed, the whole flock take wing together, and, wheeling along in half circles near the edge or the surface of the water, each bird exhibits alternately a dark or light appearance to the observer, as the upper or under side of its body happens to be turned towards him."

The *Terns*, or Sea Swallows, by their very graceful form and rapid flight, skimming along the surface of the sea, seldom fail to attract the notice of the most casual visitor. But it is not till we examine them minutely that we are aware of the numerous species which inhabit different parts of our coasts, each no doubt selecting that place where he finds ground best fitted to his wants. No less than eleven species of Tern either visit or breed on some part of the British shore. Many of them migrate to very distant places in their winter rambles, exploring the shores of tropical countries, and even extending their flights to high latitudes in the southern hemisphere. No birds are better fitted to remain long on the wing. The elegant, boat-shaped body, small in proportion to the great length of wing, is easily supported in the air during a very long-continued flight. To the same family of birds belong the Sea Gulls, which are mostly of larger size and less slender form, but with very similar habits; and also the famous *Albatross*, whose lengthy flight, reported by voyagers as continued for weeks or months together, is so celebrated. But the time which the Albatross can remain on the wing has, I think, been much exaggerated. Like the Gull and the Tern, though not a diving bird, it swims with great buoyancy, and, notwithstanding the enormous length of its wings, it does not appear to find much difficulty in mounting again in the air, after it has alighted on the water. It is quite true that when caught, and liberated on the deck of a ship, it finds it impossible to take wing: and hence it has been hastily inferred that, unless from some cliff or projection of considerable elevation, the Albatross cannot commence its flight ; and as the same birds are often found following the ship for many weeks together, it has been said that they continue all that time on the wing. But no one can have watched the Albatross with much attention, and not seen it alight frequently on the water. It lives on animal matter, which it finds floating on the sea ; and though it sometimes secures its food while on the wing by skimming along the water, it is just as common to see it close its wings and swim like a Gull: and when it wishes again to rise, it may be seen running and flapping along till it has acquired sufficient impetus, and finds a wave of sufficient height to start from. Then, with a not ungraceful motion, it soon resumes that steady flight, which may continue over a wide extent of sea.

The foot-prints of sea-birds on the sands of the shore are often unnoticed, and are swept away by the first returning wave. So are the tracks of trailing shell-fish, which may sometimes be seen furrowing the surface of fine hard sand in considerable numbers. The Common Yellow Nerite (*Littorina litoralis*) is a frequent maker of these trails, as it moves its station from one small rock to another, patiently cutting a road through the sands as it proceeds on its journey. These marks, and the undulations left by the water on the surface, where regular minute ridges of sand follow each other in an orderly manner, like the furrows in a field, appear of so fugacious a nature as to be undeserving of notice. The retreating wave has left them behind, and the returning will sweep them away, and all be a smooth surface again. Yet, in these fugitive markings of the sand the geologist traces a resemblance which links them with time immeasurably distant in the past history of the world, and with impressions on rocks which have outlived the decay of centuries, but which were, in their origin, of no more apparent stability than these marks in the sand, or than our own foot-prints. When a surface of sandstone-rock is uncovered, it very frequently exhibits markings of a nature precisely similar to what we every day meet with on the sandy shore. There is the *ripple-mark*, defined with equal regularity and sharpness — we see where every wavelet of the antediluvian ocean did its work;—there are the sinuous roads, cut out by the antediluvian molluscs, now visible in relief, by the mud which has silted into them;—the worm-like heaps of sand, which mark the position of the worm, or of the testaceous mollusc, are equally obvious in the sandstone, and on the recent shore;—the very rain-drops which impressed the sandy surface thousands of years ago have left their record on the surface of the rock. When we see all these appearances on the newly turned-up rock, and find similar markings on the flat sands of the sea, it is impossible to avoid connecting the two observations, and admitting that, in what passes under our eyes as a daily occurrence on the sands, we find the explanation of the geological phenomenon. The sandstone-rock, hard as it now may be, was once a beach, as impressible as that in which we may now be leaving our foot-prints. And though, in thousands of cases, these foot-prints will be swept away by the next flow of the water, it may so happen that they will remain. And it is a wonderful circumstance that all trace of some of the gigantic animals which once inhabited the world has perished from the knowledge of mankind, save only the track of their foot-prints left in what was then adhesive mud, but which successive ages have converted into hard stone. If Robinson Crusoe was powerfully affected by meeting with the naked human foot-print in the sand, what a crowd of thoughts are awakened by discovering in the hard rock this only evidence of a gigantic animal! A true poet has said,

> "It is the soul that sees: the outward eyes,
> Present the object, but the mind descries;
> And thence delight, disgust, or cool indiff'rence rise."

We may live among the grandest scenes of Nature, or may visit the noblest monuments of art, and remain insensible to their beauty or sublimity. Differently affected, we may find in the barren sands of the seashore enjoyment of the purest character, and speculations, which, rising from nothing more important than the train of a sea-slug, will lead us to contemplate, and in measure, to comprehend some of the most extensive operations of Nature, bringing under review unnumbered ages, past, present, and to come.

It is common to find on the sands the remains of Oyster-shells, so completely riddled with holes as to present the aspect of a pearly lacework, merely recalling by its general contour the form of the original shell, but retaining few of its characters. Meeting with such worm-eaten shells, many persons will pass them by without paying the slightest attention, or, at most, will honour them with but a heedless glance. Others may confine their reveries to recollections of Oyster-suppers. But it is just in proportion as our knowledge of Natural History extends, and as a taste for it exists in the mind, that such an object is capable of interesting us. Simple and common as it appears, a long chapter might be written in merely recording the history of its inhabitant from the time when it lay quietly on its bed among other Oysters, lodged in its firmly-built house, and appearing to defy all intruders, to the present dismantled state of the shell, resembling a ruined fortress, pierced in all directions with cannon shot. The number of enemies which the Oyster meets with, that gradually overcome his defences by mining in his shells, is considerable, not to speak of those who attack him in front :—and no doubt the dilapidated example before us is the work of several sets of teeth. His first assailants were probably small sea-worms of the class of *Annelides*, several kinds of which, some of them of great beauty, may often be seen crawling among Oysters when brought to table. These, boring through the shell, attacked him at all points. At first he resisted their assault by fresh depositions of pearly matter, interposed between his soft parts and their intruding mouths, and thus pearls were cast in the path of the enemy. But alas! they were offered to a swinish multitude, who turned aside to renew the attack on an unprotected point, till the poor Oyster's strength was well nigh exhausted in the struggle. Then, in the holes pierced by the Annelides a parasitic sponge (*Halichondria celata*) probably established itself, which ate further into his vitals, causing the softer parts of the shell to rot away, and spreading through its whole substance, like the dry-rot fungus through a solid beam of timber, until, under his accumulated misfortunes, the poor Oyster perished, and his loosened shell was cast to the mercy of the waves.

Before describing the more common inhabitants of sandy shores, I shall mention two or three objects which frequently attract us on the sands, as they are wafted to our feet by the wave, or left high and dry on shore from a previous tide. The first of these are, what are called *Mermaid's Purses*, which are of two or three sorts, one or other of which is known to most children who have rambled by the sea, though many persons may not be aware of the nature of the curious object which attracts their attention. The first and largest kind is four or five inches long, and about one-and-a-half in breadth, of a dark-brown colour, and a texture between horny and membranous, with a very fibrous structure. Its form is oblong, nearly rectangular, with the angles produced into long points. This sort of Mermaid's Purse is the egg, or sheath containing the young, of the several kinds of Ray-fish or Skate, and on some parts of the coast, according to Yarrell, they are called Skate-barrows, in allusion to their resemblance in form to a four-handed barrow. In this secure case the young fish continues to live for some time, until the nourishment provided for it in the egg is exhausted, and the little creature, increased in size and strength, is able to burst the narrow enclosure, and seek his fortune in the open sea. These purses are produced at the latter end of spring, or early summer, and will then be found to contain the young fish, in various stages of growth, nicely coiled up, with his long tail bent back toward the head. At this early stage the fish bears a near resemblance to what it afterwards attains. The flat rhomboidal body, expanding at the sides into a wide winglike margin, composed of a modification of the pectoral fins, and the long and slender thorny tail are quite as striking in the young as in the old specimen. In the Ray tribe there seems no distinct head; this part and the neck, being confounded with the body and the expanded margin, forms merely a wedge-shaped anterior extremity. The mouth, and nostrils, and gill-openings, are found on the under surface, the eyes on the upper; and this separation gives the countenance that peculiar distracted expression which is so hideous. The form of the body is admirably adapted to the habits of these fishes, which live on the bottom, where they glide along with a slow motion, assisted by gentle movements of the pectoral fins. Being as flat as the surface of the ground over which they move, and nearly of the same colour, they can pursue their game with much security and at leisure. Another, and more beautiful kind of Mermaid's Purse, is the egg of the Dog-fish, a small species of Shark.

Some of the Sharks produce their young alive; others bring them forth enclosed in these cases, which are deposited by the parent in shallow parts of the sea, along the shore. They are oblong, convex at the side, semi-transparent, of a clear yellowish horn-colour, and with a firm horny texture. From each of the four angles issues a long tendril, which coils round sea-weeds or any other fixed body near which the egg may be deposited,

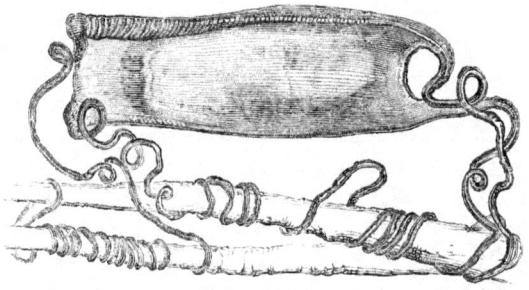

EGG OF SHARK.

and of which it can take hold; and, thus anchored, it defies securely the tossing of the waves, awaiting its proper season for being hatched. There is an opening at each end of the purse, through which the sea-water finds its way to the prisoner enclosed within, and at length the young Shark makes its exit through one of these, at the end nearest to which his head is placed.*

Another anomalous object commonly found, consists of a number of firmly membranous little bladders, each

* See Yarrell, Hist. of Brit. Fishes, 2nd edit., vol. ii. p. 487, &c.

about a quarter of an inch in breadth, flat on the inside, and convex on the outside, adhering together in regular order by their expanded margins: the whole forming a body which looks like a wasp's nest. In March or April, each of these little membranous sacs, which is found empty and pierced with a hole a month or two later, contains a soft yolk, in which is gradually formed a young univalve mollusc, whose shell begins to take its proper shape before he emerges from the membranous egg. These froth-like masses are indeed the eggs of the large Whelk (*Buccinum undatum*), which inhabits deeper water, beyond the recess of the tide, where it attaches these masses of eggs to rocks and stones, from which they often become loosened and are cast up in rough weather, as are also the Whelks themselves, whose dead shells we frequently meet with on shore. Somewhat similar eggs are produced by other allied species, the forms and localities differing in each. The eggs of a common species, with a coarse, white shell, sometimes banded with brown and yellow (*Purpura lapillus*), are frequently seen attached to small stones, on the sides of rocky hollows. These are little oblong urns, each raised on a short stalk, fixed to a circular expanded base, and pierced by a hole. They generally

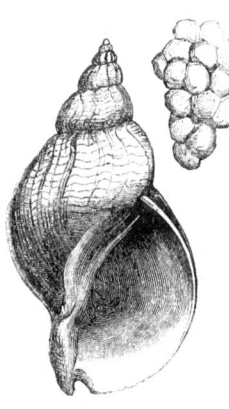

BUC. UNDATUM AND NEST.

EGGS OF MOLLUSCA.

occur in groups of ten, twenty, or more together. The egg-clusters of other Univalve Mollusca are equally curious, but they are commonly found in deeper water, or may more properly be noticed when speaking of the rocks. These animals are much more frequent on rocky ground, and naturally prefer the stability of a fixed nursery, such as a rock affords, to deposit their eggs. But one species of Sea-snail (*Natica monilifera*), with a polished, light-brown shell, elegantly marked with dark streaks and spots, either leaves its egg-cluster loose,

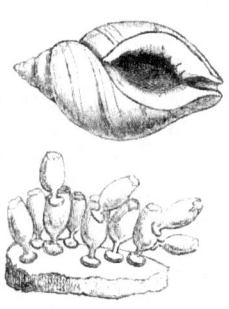

PURP. LAPILLUS AND EGGS.

in sandy places, or attaches it so carelessly that it frequently becomes loose. These egg-clusters are really very curious and elegantly-formed objects, which must have often attracted the notice of a rambler, who felt puzzled to know what they were. They are firmly gelatinous, or of the consistence of gristle; transparent, or nearly so; slightly coated

NATICA MONILIFERA.

with fine sand, and in shape resemble the hoof of an animal. When dry, they look not unlike pieces of thin Scotch oaten-bread. Their surface is marked with little hexagonal spaces, which define the eggs. But what is most to be admired in the structure, is the form of the curves which the hoof-like body assumes, which fit it for lying on loose sand, without becoming deeply buried in it. It is difficult to make this peculiar form clearly understood by mere description, but I have said sufficient to identify the object.

The Mollusca which inhabit sandy shores habitually, and in the greatest numbers, are not the *Univalve* or snail-like families, whose organization is more adapted for crawling over rocks and sea-plants, where also they find their appropriate food ;—but another very distinct group of shell-coated animals, called CONCHIFERA,* or TESTACEOUS ACEPHALA, which are capable of living buried, sometimes to a considerable depth in the sands. Some of this class of animals are indeed confined to rocky places, anchoring themselves in various ways permanently in a position, either on a rock or on the stem of a sea-weed ; or forming hollow chambers by burrowing in the solid rock itself ; but the majority of species inhabit sandy places, and their shells continually meet us on the sandy shore, while the living animals may be detected buried along the margin of the retreated tide. The shell, in all these animals, consists of two principal, saucer-shaped pieces, more or less perfectly covering the body of the animal, and united together by a more or less complex hinge, opened by a highly-elastic ligament. The *Scallop* and the *Common Cockle* offer well-known examples of such a shell:—the first having a simpler structure, both in the hinge and in the animal, is better adapted for explaining the general features of organi-

* " General Outlines of the Animal Kingdom, by Professor Rymer Jones," p. 375, *et seq.*

zation, while the latter may be instanced as affording modifications of structure which adapt it to the peculiar locality to which it is confined.

On opening the valves of a living Scallop we perceive, within the margin of the shell, a soft membrane, which lines the whole of the inner surface, and encloses the body of the animal as in a cloak, open in front through the centre; so that a curtain fringed round the edge with innumerable slender filaments, hangs from each valve of the shell. This membranous envelope, which is called the *mantle*, exists, though under many modifications, in all the Mollusca, and indeed is one of their most essential parts. It is by means of this organ that all the shell-coated tribes cover themselves with the beautiful shells which are objects of so general admiration. The thickened margin of the mantle is furnished with glands which secrete both colouring-matter and carbonate of lime. From the latter material, deposited in cellular substance derived from the animal, the shell is gradually formed by constant additions to its margin; while the colouring-matter, poured in at the same time, gives to the outer surface all the peculiar markings which characterize each kind. The outer coat of the shell is therefore entirely the work of the margin of the mantle. Its increase in thickness is an after-process, effected by the general surface of this organ, which throws off layers of pearly substance, and adds them continually, one after another, to the inner surface of the shell. Thus, as the shell increases in size, its walls grow in thickness. In the Scallop, among the fringing processes of the margin, are found a number of glittering studs of metallic brilliancy, which are supposed to be eyes—and at least are the only representative of those organs observed in the class, whose habits little require such a provision. Within the mantle are found the branchiæ or lungs, which consist of four delicate leaves formed of radiating fibres of extreme fineness. The *mouth* is a simple orifice, bordered by membranous lips, and placed at one end of the body, between the two inner leaves of the branchiæ. A great portion of the body consists of an extremely firm muscle, round which the stomach, liver, and other parts, are disposed, and which connects the two valves of the shell together; by its expansion allowing them to open, and causing them to close by its contraction. This most powerful muscle alone keeps the shell closed; and its strength must be familiar to every one who has opened an Oyster, whose resistance to the knife ceases only when this muscle is cut asunder.

Such are the general features of the more simple conchiferous animals, as the Scallop and Oyster. If we examine the Cockle, we shall find some modifications, and the full developement of a highly-organized muscular foot. This organ exists but in a rudimentary form in the Scallop, whose habits suggest other modes of locomotion than those of running and leaping. The Scallop, which inhabits deep places, where it lies on a rocky or shelly bottom, swims or *flies* through the water with great rapidity, moving itself by suddenly opening and shutting the valves. In the Cockle the first difference which strikes us is, that the edges of the mantle are not open all round, as in the Scallop, but united together, at one side, into a short tube. On cutting a little deeper we perceive that the shell is held together by *two* muscles, one placed on each side of the central hinge. The hinge itself is differently formed, the *ligament* which connects the valves being external, and the joint furnished with a nicely-fitted apparatus of tooth-like plates. On the whole, we have a higher type of structure, while the developement of a large muscular foot, capable of being either wholly retracted within the shell or protruded to a considerable length, marks a new feature in the animal, which at once suggests a difference in habits and destiny. That the differences observed in the organization of the Cockle, and of the allied genera, *Mactra*, *Venus*, &c., and which are found in a still more advanced state in the *Myæ* or Gapers, and the *Solen* or Razor-shell, admirably fit them for the sphere of life for which they are designed, is at once obvious when we consider these modifications of structure in reference to the habitat of the animal.

All these animals inhabit sandy or muddy places. Their dead shells are among the commonest which we meet with on almost every strand; and they may be found in a living state, near low-water-mark, buried in holes, which reveal themselves by slight depressions, from which little jets of sand and water may, every now and then, be seen to issue. For such a life as this their organization peculiarly fits them. Were their mantle open on all sides, like that of the Scallop, their branchiæ would soon become choked with the sand or mud, which would have free entrance with the water received into the shell, and thus the animal would quickly be suffocated. But the tubular opening through which the currents of water enter effectually protects the delicate breathing-apparatus. Their strong muscular foot, too, affords an instrument with which they can with great rapidity dig into the sand, and thus escape pursuit. So rapidly is this mining operation performed, that it requires some dexterity and quickness to surprise even a Cockle in its hole, before it has burrowed beyond our reach. But it is not as a digging-tool only that the foot is employed; it is used in actual locomotion on the surface, to enable the animal either to advance with a crawling movement, or to make jumps along the sand. The Common Cockle is not the least nimble of these jumpers. It protrudes its foot to the utmost length, bending it and fixing it strongly against the surface on which it stands, and then, by a sudden muscular spring, the animal throws itself into the air, and by repeating the process again and again, it hops along at a rapid pace. In the Cockle, which lives at no great depth in the sand, the cohesion of the two membranes of the mantle is not complete, and the tubes or *siphons* are very short. In other genera, as the Razor-shells, which burrow to a greater depth, the lateral cohesion is much more perfect. The body of the animal is enclosed in a sort of sac, while the tubes, through which currents of water enter to the branchiæ are much protruded. The animal can thus lie deeply ensconced in the sand or mud, and keep the mouths of the tubes nearly on a level with the surface of the sand, in direct communication with the water.

The mode in which all the animals of this class feed

is not the least curious part of their history. They subsist, for the most part, like vegetables, without the trouble of seeking for prey. It is brought to the door of their shells, and they have but to " gape and swallow it." The water which enters at the openings in the mantle brings in with it nourishing particles of one kind or other, minute animals, &c. These, floating about in the shell, come under the influence of millions of minute *cilia* or vibratory hairs which clothe every part of the branchial-fringe, and which, by their constant motion, form a current strong enough to drive forward to the mouth whatever is floating in the water. The food is thus presented to the lips, which have only to decide whether to receive it or let it pass into the influence of the retreating current, which will carry it out of the shell. To so low a type is animal *will* reduced in these passionless creatures, which, nevertheless, exhibit the most wonderful perfection in the construction of their minutest organs, and the most beautiful adaptations of means to ends. The beauty of the shells of many of them is apparent to all—the graceful forms of many species of *Venus* and *Chione*,—the rich colouring of the *Pectens*, the *Spondyli*, and *Tellinæ*—but all these beauties are less impressive to the mind than the exquisite structure of the *mantle* by which these shells are secreted, and the admirable order with which the very particles of the shells are arranged: an order so exact, that the *species* to which a *minute fragment* of a shell belongs may often be determined, or approximated to, by making a microscopic examination of thinly-cut slices. Thus, an examination of shelly particles, no bigger than grains of sand, may reveal to the naturalist much of the history of the shell of which it is the *débris*.* The importance of such a fact to the geologist is obvious, but I speak of it here chiefly as affording an instance of the wonderful skill with which these humble works of an unseen Worker are constructed. " Lo, these are parts of His ways, but how little a portion is heard of Him!"†

In the scientific classification, or the division into genera, of bivalve shells, the most important characters derivable from the shell are to be found in the modifications of the teeth and ligaments of the hinge, the position of the impressions of the adductor-muscle, and of the line which marks the adherence of the mantle with the shell. The first of these characters forms the basis of the Linnæan genera. In the simpler forms of hinge, as in the Oyster, the Scallop, and the Mussel, there are no teeth, the hinge consisting of a ligament, either sunk into a triangular pit, or forming a marginal line extending along the shell. The first step in advance of this structure is found in the *Mya*, or Gaper, where a single spoon-shaped tooth receives the ligament. From this upward, through *Lutraria, Mactra, Cardium*, &c., we are conducted to exceedingly complicated dental processes; till we find in *Arca* and its allies an infinity of sharp teeth, like those of a pair of combs, fitting accurately into each other. In most genera the number and position of the teeth are nearly the same in all the species. But in a very natural

* See Dr. Carpenter's paper on this subject in Report of British Association, 1847. † Job xxvi. 14.

group, the genus *Lucina*, there is less uniformity in
the hinge than usual; and here we gladly have recourse
to the impression of the adductor-muscles, one
of which, in this genus, is prolonged in a remarkable
manner. The impression of the mantle appears also to
afford excellent generic characters, though it has only
recently been admitted by conchologists into their descriptions.
It may be observed, on the inside of each
valve, forming a narrow line, more glossy than the rest
of the shell, connecting one muscular impression with
the other. It forms different curves in different genera,
and exhibits many minor variations. But our limits
do not permit us to consider the niceties of classification,
and we must refer for further information on
the subject to Messrs. Forbes' and Hanley's History of
the British Mollusca.

Much lower in the scale of being than *Bivalve*
Mollusca, but elaborately organized, and offering many
interesting points in their history, are the Heart
Urchins, a tribe of animals enclosed in egg-like shells,
coated with spines, which inhabit all our sandy bays.
There are several recent British species, but I shall
only mention the common Heart Urchin (*Amphidotus cordatus*),
Mermaid's Head, or Sea Egg, as it is
variously called, which is found all round the coast.
When alive, it is thickly clothed with fine hair-like
spines, each of which is articulated at base with a minute
nipple, forming a ball-and-socket joint, so that
the spine can move freely in all directions. The spines
are of different forms and length on different parts of
the body, and, frail as they appear, serve the purpose to

which they are applied, of enabling the animal to sink itself in the sand, shovelling the fine particles out of the way, and throwing them over its back. When thrown upon shore, the spines are usually more or less broken, and soon are completely worn off, when the dead shell resembles a heart-shaped egg, of a dirty-white colour, frosted over with minute tubercles, which are largest on its under surface, where the orifice of the mouth is seen; and it is marked, both on the back and lower surface, with five radiating smooth depressions, bordered with a double row of *pin-holes*. These spaces, which are much more developed on the back than on the oral surface, are called *ambulacra;* and through the pores or *pin-holes* which border them, the animal protrudes long worm-like suckers, which serve the office of feet, and enable him to move about by a sort of *warping* motion (to speak nautically), fixing the sucker of one fibrous cord in advance of his position, gradually bringing the rest forward, and so dragging the body along. Those on the oral surface are much less developed, and chiefly serve to hold the ground. It is curious to find a creature whose organs of locomotion are most developed on the upper surface; but we may be assured that they are not so placed without a wise design. It is easy to see that such an organization enables the creature to recover its natural position with ease, if accidentally inverted; but the arrangement probably serves many other purposes.

The affinity of the *Heart Urchin* with the common *Egg Urchins* is readily seen; their connexion with *Star-fishes* is, at first sight, less obvious. Nevertheless, a careful comparison of the living animals will show many points in common:—thus the five-rayed *ambulacra* on the back of the *Amphidotus* represent the rays of the Star-fish; and when we place a large number of species, recent and fossil, under review, the passage from the most branching Star-fish to the roundest Sea Egg may be clearly made out through a beautiful gradation of forms. We shall have occasion, probably, to return to the subject in a subsequent chapter. The family of *Echinidæ*, to which these animals belong, was much richer in forms in the earlier world than it at present appears to be; and from the great facility with which the hard parts of the shelly integument may be preserved, the remains of these creatures have come down to us in a very perfect state. The study of them, therefore, is quite as interesting to the geologist as to the zoologist. It is of importance to the former to know the habits of the living species, that he may form a judgment on what those of the extinct kinds may have been, and thus arrive at just conclusions on the circumstances under which the rocks and gravels, where their remains are preserved, have been deposited. Of the sub-tribe of Heart Urchins (*Spatangaceæ*), very numerous species, many of them of highly curious and elegant forms, exist in the oolite and the chalk, and abound in many tertiary deposits. They all characterise marine strata, and generally indicate shallow parts of the sea. Very few of the kinds now living have been found fossilized, except in deposits which are evidently of a very recent date. Thus in these, as in other races of animals, there have been successions of species, each marking its own era.

Among the common productions of sandy shores several species of Zoophytes present themselves, generally in a dead state, the fleshy parts having wholly disappeared, leaving merely the skeleton or skin behind. These skeletons often resemble sea-weeds, both in the plant-like forms they assume, and in bearing along the branches little membranous sacs, which look like minute flowers or seed-vessels, and are, indeed, organs of a similar nature, being the ovaries in which the germs of the young Polypes are contained. From sea-weeds the skeletons in question may always be known by their horny or bony texture, and their generally pale, testaceous colour. There is but one group of sea-plants, the jointed corallines, which so far resemble some of them in being hard, and indeed stony in substance, as to lead to their being commonly confounded, even by naturalists,

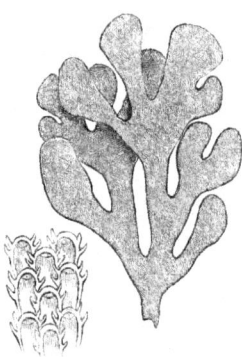

FLUSTRA FOLIACEA.

with skeletons of Zoophytes. But these are rock-plants, which we shall speak of in another chapter. Most of the Zoophytes, also, are natives of rocky places, or of shingly ground, such as oyster-beds, beyond the reach of the tide. And it is only the species which are accidentally thrown up by the waves which we meet with on strands. Of these, one of the most common is *Flustra foliacea*, represented in the annexed cut, a much-branched species, of a papery substance and dirty-white colour, flat, and built up of innumerable little oblong cells, placed back to back, like those of a honey-comb, and each crowned (as may readily be seen with the help of a pocket-lens) by four stout spines. It is these spines which give the surface of the *Polypidom* (as the plant-like body is called) its peculiar, rough, or harsh feel, observable if the finger be passed over the surface from the apex towards the base.

This structure of cells (*polypidom* or leafy-body) is not the remains of a single animal, but of a community of individuals as numerous as those of one of our cities, each of which dwelt within the narrow compass of one of the cells, in which he was born, lived, and died. This cell was his house, more literally his skin, within which he enjoyed an independent existence, at the same time that he was linked, by a common circulation, to the cells above and below him; and thus had a double existence, being at the same time himself, and a part of " the neighbours;" or rather, a part of the compound animal represented by the polypidom itself, and whose individuality is exhibited by the regularity of its growth; just as a plant, which may be considered as a community of separate leaves, proves its individuality by the orderly manner in which those leaves are arranged. The life enjoyed by this common *Flustra* may be taken as an example of that of a class of animals to which it is related, the compound Polypes whose remains, recent and fossil, constitute an enormous portion of the fossilized crust of the earth. The general form and structure of the individual Polypes may be illustrated by the largest members of the group, the Sea Anemones, whose flower-like bodies are seen expanded in every rock-pool left by the tide. The little Polypes which dwelt in the cells of the *Flustra* were animals of a something similar form, though different structure, each crowned with a star-like flower; and the whole together exhaled an odour, when fresh, compared by some observers to that of the orange, by others to that of violets, and, again, to a mixture of the odour of roses and geranium.* The sea has its gardens as well as the land, and their denizens more wonderful, for the flowers of the sea enjoy animal life.

It is common, in speaking of coral-banks and islands, to attribute the formation of these vast submarine deposits to the work of the Polypes, and to extol the industry of the little creatures in building up monuments whose vastness leaves the pyramids an immeasurable distance behind. And, in some sense indeed, coral-islands are their work; but scarcely in a higher sense than peat-bogs may be seen to be the work of mosses, or the coal-fields those of other classes of vegetables. In speaking of coral-islands as the work of the Polypes, we lose sight of the fact that the island itself is one vast polypidom, all whose living parts have, in the aggregate, as much individuality—so far as they consist of a single species—as the polypidom of the *Flustra* we have been examining. In coral-banks several species unite together, and each, of course, preserves its individuality; but it is quite conceivable to suppose a single species, forming a single mass, and gradually constituting a

---

* See Johnston's Brit. Zoop. 2nd. Edit., p. 342-3.

ALCYONIUM DIGITATUM.

bank or island. Now, the growth of the insular mass no more depends on the will of the Polypes, of whose branches it consists, than the growth of any other skeleton depends on the will of the animal whose organs secrete it.

A very common Zoophyte, frequently thrown up on sandy shores from deep water, very different in aspect from the *Flustra*, but belonging to a neighbouring family of animals, is what is commonly called Dead-men's Toes or Hands (*Alcyonium digitatum*). This constitutes a fleshy semi-transparent mass, coated with a tough orange-coloured skin and exceedingly sportive in shape: sometimes forming a mere crust on the surface of the shell to which it adheres; at other times pushing up a trunk which divides into finger-like branches. As it lies on the shore it certainly offers few inducements, from its beauty, to recommend it to further notice; yet it is one of the many natural productions which only require to be looked at with a moderate attention to elicit from them much that is curious and beautiful in structure. If a piece

ALCYONIUM DIGITATUM.

of this Zoophyte, newly cast up, be placed in a vessel of sea-water, it will soon acquire favour in our eyes. The tough, orange skin, when closely looked at, will be found studded with innumerable star-like points, each furnished with eight rays, and marking the orifice of the cell in which a Polype is lodged. When the polypidom has remained a while in the water, its Polypes, if still alive, will gradually protrude themselves from the starry points, pushing out a cylindrical body, clear as crystal, fluted like a column, and terminated by a flower-like, eight-rayed mouth; the whole surface, at last, becoming densely clothed with these animated flowers. The unsightly aspect of the trunk, which reminded us of fingers or toes, is now forgotten, just as we forget the fleshy branches of a cactus when we see it clothed with its gorgeous flowers. Nor is the internal structure of our Zoophyte less worthy of examination and admiration. Not to speak of its minute anatomy, a simple longitudinal section, if examined with a moderate lens, will reveal a complicated system of inosculating canals, which form a sort of circulation through the mass, by connecting with the rest of the body the Polype-cells, which are placed immediately under the outer skin. These tubes are bound together by a fibrous network, and lie imbedded in a transparent jelly, which forms the fleshy part of the compound animal. The eggs are lodged in the tubes, and at length discharged through the mouth. Such is the simple structure of these animals, which are nevertheless arranged with as much care and nicety, in proportion to their organization, as we find in animals much higher in the scale of being.

The marine plants which occupy sandy shores are not numerous, though a great variety of beautiful kinds may often be picked up on the beach after a gale. These come from deeper water, either where the sand is more firmly compacted than on the shore, or where masses of rock interrupt its continuity, and afford a site for a colony of sea-weeds. One marine plant, however, the only British instance of a flowering plant inhabiting the sea, frequently forms extensive submarine meadows on sandy shores. This is the Grass Wrack (*Zosteramarina*), whose creeping stems, rooting at the joints, admirably fit it for establishing itself on loose sands, and forming the nucleus of a soil in which other plants may grow. Its long, riband-like leaves, of a brilliant green colour and satiny lustre, waving freely in the water, afford shelter and nourishment to a host of marine animals and plants. Great numbers of epiphytic sea-weeds of small size, but many of them of exquisite beauty, may be collected on the leaves of *Zostera*, which are frequented also by numerous Zoophytes, and by the smaller gasteropodous Mollusca. A *Zostera*-bed is therefore always worth examining. But it is chiefly when the *Zostera* grows beyond the reach of the tide, and is raised by dragging hooks through it, that it is found so well clothed with Sea-weeds and Zoophytes. Nearer shore it frequently collects muddy particles, which defile all that grows upon it. This plant is collected on many parts of the coast, and even imported in large quantities from the Baltic, being sold, under the market name of *Alva marina*, to the manufacturers of cheap bedding. It is said to form a very tolerable bed, and certainly a cheap one. It also makes an excellent material for packing glass and earthenware.

But it is time to take leave of the productions of the sandy shore, and explore those that seek a firmer footing on submarine rocks, the truly prolific soil of the sea. I pass by the intermediate stages of shingly shores, and shores covered with boulders, neither of which are favourable to the growth of marine plants, or the sheltering of animals. On loose-lying boulders few sea-weeds, except *Fucus nodosus*, a coarse leathery species, with large air-bladders, and a few unsightly *Ulvæ*, are found ; while the animals are restricted to the Common Limpet, and the least attractive of the Sea Anemones (*Actinia Mesembryanthemum*), with scabby patches of *Balani* and Mussels, a few Periwinkles, &c. By exploring the smaller stones lying on such a shore, many curious Annelides and small Molluscs, small Crabs, &c. may be captured ; and, therefore, these shores should not be neglected by the naturalist : but the labour is often disproportionate to the value of the crop he may expect to reap. The study of such beaches will, however, always interest the geologist whose speculations take a wider range, and who finds, in the slowly changing character of such a beach, the explanation of many of the appearances presented to him on land. The gradual formation and accumulation of gravel by the action of water, and the commencement of conglomerate rocks, are often beautifully exhibited. Nor must the *débris* of marine shells, &c., which marks the limits of ordinary tides, be omitted in the general survey. It is curious to watch the gradual formation of beds of these remains, and to trace them, as may frequently be done, above the present sea-mark, into fossil-beds filled with the remains of existing species. Following up these deposits further, we gradually find, by the introduction of new forms which no longer exist in a living state on our shores, that we are challenging the videttes which stand sentinel to another territory, inhabited by a different race of beings. And thus we are led, step by step, and often insensibly, far back into the dreamy regions of the early history of our planet; into times and seasons when the sun looked down on no dwelling of man, but when his beams gave life to countless tribes of creatures whose race is now run, and whose half-told tale is found written in the earth or the rock. If their race be extinct and their glory departed, at least they live in marble, and human greatness can often boast no more. Finally, we reach a time when the waves of a primeval sea sounded hollow on a naked shore, and no ear listened to their music.

> "Sky, sun, and sea, were all the universe;
> The sky, one blue interminable arch,
> Without a breeze, a wing, a cloud: the sun
> Sole in the firmament, but in the deep
> Redoubled; where the circle of the sea,
> Invisible with calmness, seemed to lie,
> Within the hollow of a lower heaven."
>
> MONTGOMERY.

TOR ABBEY ROCKS AND HEADLAND, WITH BERRY HEAD IN THE DISTANCE.

CHAPTER III.

THE ROCKY SEA-SHORE ;—SEA-WEEDS.

THE success of a marine-botanist, or *Algologist*, on a rocky coast will depend more on the extent of surface uncovered at low-water-mark, and on the outward conformation of the rocks of which the tidal margin is composed, than on the geological structure of the district. Soil in some measure affects the vegetation of the sea, but not to any great extent. The roots of sea-plants bear little resemblance to those of land-plants. Few are fibrous, and few indeed send out extensive bundles of fibres to seek through a varying soil the substances necessary for their perfect growth. The roots of sea-weeds must be regarded more in the nature of holdfasts, destined to keep the vegetable fixed in a proper locality, than as separate organs contributing to the nourishment of the body. With this end in view, Nature furnishes sea-weeds, in the great majority of instances, with a simple conical disc, by which they strongly adhere to the smoothest surface; and when a more root-like holdfast

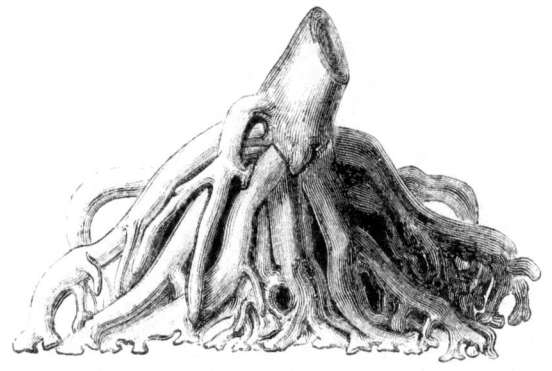

ROOT OF LAMINARIA.

is given, it is merely a multiplication of such discs, or a strengthening by lateral ropes the original gripe taken of the rock. Roots of this nature may be seen in the large Oar-weeds (*Laminariæ*) of our coasts, particularly in the *L. digitata*, a species with a long cylindrical walking-stick-stem, crowned with a broad leaf, cloven into a great number of ribbon-like segments. In this plant, while young, the root consists of a few rudimentary processes:—as it advances in growth, and as new props are required to support the additional weight, the branches of the root lengthen and others are gradually added, till a compact mass of interwoven fibres is formed, each of which takes a separate gripe of the rock, by the disc at its extremity, and all combined form a conical mass, representing the simple disc of the *Fuci* and most other sea-weeds. On some sandy shores, there are sea-weeds with much more extensive roots,—roots that resemble those of grasses which cover sand-downs, extending to a considerable depth in the sand, branching out in every direction, and forming a compact bed of fibres, and a firm foundation for the vegetation. Such roots are obviously induced by the nature of the soil on which the plant grows, and would be superfluous on a rocky bottom.

The roots of sea-weeds seem to be little concerned in the active growth of the vegetable, except in the earlier stages. Like all the lower vegetables included in the class *Cryptogamia*, the sea-weeds are composed of a simple aggregation of cells,* which form a more or less homogeneous body through which fluids freely pass, and whose whole surface absorbs nourishment from the surrounding water. This is the reason why the geological nature of the district has little relation to that of the marine vegetation which clothes the rocks. But the character of this vegetation is greatly varied by the outward form of the rocky masses. Thus, on a shore composed of granite-rocks, where the masses are rounded and

---

* A *cell*, in botanical language, means a little bag-like body, composed of membrane, and containing a living substance capable of spontaneous growth by multiplication or division of its parts. Of such little bodies, millions of which may be contained within a cubic inch, all the soft parts of vegetables are composed. In sea-weeds the cells are often of large size.

lumpy, with few interstices or cavities in which water will constantly lie; and presenting to the waves sloping ridges, along which the water freely runs up and down, very few species of sea-weeds, and these only of the coarsest kinds, are commonly to be met with. And thus the vegetation of granitic shores may be characterised as poor. But this poverty is owing altogether to outward form. For, wherever the granite affords a tolerably flat surface, interspersed with deep cavities in which pools of water are constantly maintained, a vegetation will be found as varied and copious as on stratified shores of a totally different composition of rock. The best localities are those in which there are the greatest number of rock-pools of moderate extent, with perpendicular sides, and a depth varying from one to three feet. Pools of this character, though situated near high-water-mark, so as to communicate with the sea only when the tide is near its height, often produce all the species which are considered to be characteristic of extreme low-water-mark. Their depth is sufficient to keep the water at a sufficiently even temperature, and their steep sides afford that shade which the more delicate sea-weeds require. On chalky shores I have observed that sea-weeds are poor, and few in number. And this I attribute chiefly to the general absence of such rock-pools, though no doubt the soft nature of the rock has its influence, and the white surface, reflecting a greater quantity of light than the more delicate *Floridea* can endure, drives such species to a greater depth of water on chalky shores than on others, and thus beyond the influence of the tide, or the reach of the botanist. The frequent occurrence of favourable aspects on shores composed of sandstone, or of clay-slate — and the colour of these rocks, render such shores the most prolific in species.

I shall now take a rapid survey of the vegetation which characterises what is termed the *littoral zone*,* or that belt of rock or shingle which extends from high-water to low-water-mark. Within this space a large proportion of the sea-weeds of our latitude is produced; and the remainder, with the exception of a few stragglers that extend into deeper water, occur within the limit of two, or, at most, of four fathoms beyond the lowest water of spring-tides.

Sea-weeds are usually classed by botanists in three great groups, each of which contains several families, which are again divided into genera; and these, in their turn, are composed of one or many species. The number of species as yet detected on the British coasts is about 370, and they are grouped into 105 genera. I cannot, in this place, enter into the niceties of classification to which botanists resort in working out the history of these plants, but must confine myself to the general features of the great groups, and their distribution. Taken in the order in which they present themselves to us on the shore, and limiting each by its most obvious character, that of colour, we may observe:—that the group of Green Sea-weeds (*Chlorospermeæ*) abound near high-water-mark, and in shallow tide-pools within the tidal limit;—that the Olive-coloured (*Melanospermeæ*) cover all exposed rocks, feebly commencing at

---

* See Prof. Edward Forbes, in Geol. Surv. Memoirs.

the margin of high-water, and increasing in luxuriance with increasing depth, through the whole belt of exposed rock;—but that the majority of them cease to grow soon after they reach a depth which is never laid bare to the influence of the atmosphere:—and that the Red Sea-weeds (*Rhodospermeæ*) gradually increase in numbers, and in purity of colour, as they recede from high-water-mark, or grow in places where they enjoy a perfect shade, or nearly total absence of light, and are never exposed to the air, or subjected to a violent change of temperature.

The Green Sea-weeds are the simplest in structure, and the least varied in species, on different coasts, and consequently the least interesting to the collector of specimens. With the exception of the beautiful genus *Cladophora*, which contains about twenty species, our British *Chlorosperms* are chiefly composed of *Ulvæ* and *Enteromorphæ*, whose forms vary with so little order, that it becomes difficult, and, in some instances, hopeless, to attempt to classify the varieties. The *Enteromorphæ* are the first to make their appearance about high-water-mark, covering loose boulders or smooth rocks with a slippery vesture of bright green, or filling the shallow tide-pools with grassy fronds. These plants consist of tubular membranes, simple or branched, appearing to the naked eye like fine green silk, and showing to the microscope a surface composed of minute cells, full of granules. The commonest species near high-water-mark is *E. compressa*, which commences of a very stunted size, and with thread-like branches, if exposed to the air, and gradually acquires length and breadth as it grows in deeper water. When fully developed, it has a frond divided nearly to the root into many long, subsimple branches, which bear a second or third series, all of them much attenuated at their insertion, and more or less distended at the extremity. The diameter of the tube varies extremely, and the broader and simpler individuals are only to be known from *E. intestinalis*, by their being branched; the tube in the latter species being absolutely simple. To the *Enteromorphæ* succeed *Ulvæ*, distinguished from *Enteromorphæ* merely by being flat, instead of tubular. The beautiful lettuce-like plaited leaves found in tide-pools, belong to plants of this genus, the commonest species of which is *U. latissima*. It has a very broad, more or less ovate, plaited leaf, of a brilliant green, and remarkably glossy, when in perfection reflecting glaucous tints, if seen through clear sea-water, and is certainly a very ornamental species. It is sometimes brought to table as a laver, or marine sauce, but it is much inferior in flavour to the Purple Laver (*Porphyra laciniata*), a plant of the same family, equally beautiful, equally common, and more generally collected for food. The Purple Laver grows on exposed rocks near low-water-mark, and though called purple, assumes at different seasons of the year different shades of colour, according to its age. In form it resembles the Green Laver (*Ulva latissima*), but is of a still more delicate substance, consisting of a perfectly transparent and very thin membrane, elegantly dotted with closely-set grains, to which it owes its colour. When these grains are in perfection they are of a dark violet-purple; and this is the case in winter and early spring, when the plant is collected for table. Later in the year the fronds are of stunted size, and more or less olivaceous colour, and much less suitable for gathering. The plant appears to be of very rapid growth and decay, a few weeks sufficing for its full developement. Like many fugitive plants, however, it is not confined to one season, but continues to develope throughout the year; but with this difference, that the plants developed in summer are very much smaller, more tenacious, and of a dull colour. These last are regarded by some authors as a different species, and called *P. umbilicata.*

There is a circumstance connected with the history of our common *Ulvæ, Enteromorphæ,* and *Porphyræ,* which deserves notice. Most of the species common to the European shores are found in all parts of the world to which a marine vegetation extends. In the cold waters of the Arctic sea, *Ulva latissima, Enteromorpha compressa,* and *Porphyra laciniata,* vegetate in abundance; and these same plants skirt the shores of tropical seas, and extend into the southern ocean as far as Cape Horn. Vegetation, at least with its most obvious features, ceases in the south at a much lower parallel than in the Arctic regions, and the shores of the Antarctic lands appear to be perfectly barren, producing not even an *Ulva.* But the fact of the great adaptability of plants of this family to different climates, is beautifully illustrated by the last land-plant collected by the acute naturalist attached to our Antarctic expedition. The last plant that struggles with perpetual winter was gathered at

Cockburn Island, 64° S. (a latitude no greater than that of Archangel, where the vine is said to ripen in the open air), and this proved to be an

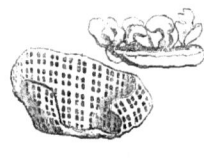

ULVA CRISPA.

Ulva (*U. crispa**), identical with a small species which may often be seen in this country on old thatch, or on damp walls and rocks, forming extensive patches of small green leaves. It is not common to find marine plants with so wide a distribution; but a nearly equal extent of sea is characterized by another of the

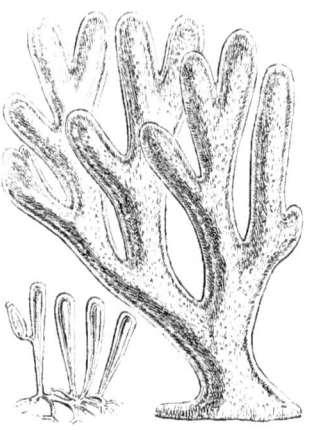

CODIUM TOMENTOSUM.

British *Chlorosperms*, of a much greater size and more complex structure. On most of the rocky coasts of Britain may be gathered, in tide-pools, or rocks near low-water-mark, an Alga of a bright green colour and spongy texture, cylindrical, and much branched, the branches dividing pretty regularly by repeated forkings, and the whole invested, when seen under water, with a downy coat of colourless filaments. The name of this plant is *Codium tomentosum*. Under the microscope it is found to be wholly composed of

* See "Flora Antarctica," vol. ii. p. 498. In the northern hemisphere, *Ulva crispa* extends to Spitzbergen, in lat. 80°.

small threads, of a tenacious, membranous consistence, filled with a dense granular fluid, closely and intricately matted together; the threads in the centre of the branches having a longitudinal direction, while those of the circumference are horizontal, presenting their closely-set tips to the surface of the frond. This plant abounds on the shores of the Atlantic, from the north of Europe to the Cape of Good Hope: it appears to be equally common in the Pacific, extending along the whole western coast of the American Continent: it is found in the Indian sea, and on the shores of Australia and New Zealand: nor is there any certain character by which the specimens of one country may be known from those of another.

Allied to the *Codium* in structure, and not uncommon in rock-pools, is a slender and extremely elegant little plant, *Bryopsis plumosa*, which consists of a multitude of soft green feathers gracefully connected together. Its substance is exceedingly flaccid, and the branches fall together when removed from the water, but immediately expand on re-immersion. Few of our marine plants are more beautiful; and the pleasure of admiring its graceful characters may be indefinitely prolonged, as it is one of the plants which may be most

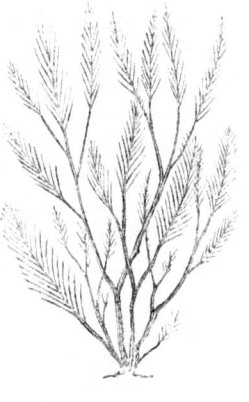

BRYOPSIS PLUMOSA.

easily grown in bottles of sea-water. Whilst it continues to vegetate, it will keep the water sweet and pure, and no care is needed except to close the mouth of the bottle, so as to prevent evaporation. The *Bryopsis*, in all its characters, has the structure of a vegetable ; nor does it much resemble the Zoophites in aspect. And yet it is one of those plants which closely link the lower members of the vegetable kingdom with those of the animal. Through *Bryopsis*, the passage is very clear into *Acetabularia*, an elegant Mediterranean plant, which closely resembles a Zoophite, and which was, indeed, till lately, classed in that division of animals. Instances of

CLADOPHORA HUTCHINSIÆ.

this kind of seeming connexion between the two great kingdoms of the organized world, meet us frequently among the lower groups of either, and often, as in this case, where connexion is least looked for. The genus *Cladophora*, to which I have already alluded, consists of the branching species of the green division of the old genus *Conferva*. These plants are formed of strings of cells, one cell growing from the apex of another, so as to form a jointed thread. The species are distinguished by differences in the branching, in the proportionate length of the cells, and in their diameter ; and nearly all of them are beautiful objects. They mostly form scattered tufts, in rock-pools, but some occur gregariously in extensive patches, covering rocks or Fuci with a bright green fringe.

I shall now notice a few of the more common of the Olive-coloured group of Sea-weeds, or *Melanospermeæ*, so called because their reproductive grains, or spores, are of a dark colour, or so opake that they appear dark when seen by transmitted light. This group consists of much more perfectly-formed plants than those we have just noticed. They are, also, commonly of much greater size: the largest of all sea-plants belong to them. The Olive Sea-weeds commence to grow, as I have already said, just within the margin of the tide, and they extend throughout the whole of the littoral zone, and to the depth of one or two fathoms below low-water-mark. The first species we meet with is *Fucus canaliculatus*, the smallest and most slender of the British Fuci. It grows in scattered tufts, one or two inches high, on rocks about high-water-mark, and is at once known by having narrow, channelled stems and branches, without air-vessels. It rarely grows in water of a greater depth than three or four feet, and never in places where it is not exposed for several hours daily to the air. To it succeed *Fucus nodosus*, a large species, with leathery, thong-like stems, distended at intervals into knob-like air-vessels, and covered in winter and spring with bright-yellow berries; and *F. vesiculosus*, a more membranous kind, having a forked leaf, traversed by a mid-rib, and bearing numerous air-vessels in pairs, at either side of the rib. This species is gregarious, covering wide patches of rock from a foot or two below high-water- to low-water-mark. Growing thus, at different times, in a very different depth of water, it varies greatly in size. The specimens found near high-water-mark are small, and generally without air-vessels, these organs not being required to float the plant in shallow water; while all that grow in deep water are abundantly provided with them, and have fronds several feet in length, that stand erect in the water, buoyed up by the air-vessels. About the level of half-tide a fourth species of Fucus makes its appearance, *Fucus serratus*, distinguished from all the rest by its toothed margin, and the absence of air-vessels. This species abounds on all the rocks to the limit of low-water, growing, like *F. vesiculosus*, in society. These four species are all the true Fuci that are common to every part of the coast, and that impart to the vegetation of the rocky sea-beach its peculiar olive-brown character. All of them, but particularly *F. serratus* and *F. vesiculosus*, are employed in the manufacture of kelp, an impure carbonate of soda, obtained by burning the dried stems of these plants. Before the alteration of the tariff, and especially in war-time, when the market was badly supplied with alkali, great revenues were obtained by the owners of rocky shores from the trade in kelp; but, now that soda is procured by an inexpensive chemical process from rock-salt, the manufacture of kelp has been much neglected, and has dwindled down to insignificance. At present the only demand for this commodity, is from the manufacturers of iodine, the chief source of that valuable substance being found in the *Algæ* of this family. It is much to be regretted that a trade, once so valuable to a large population on the western coast of Scotland and

Ireland, where the means of livelihood are scanty, should have ceased to yield a profitable return; but these are revolutions to which all manufactures are subject. At some future time other uses may be found for the abundant crop of these plants which our shores supply. At present large quantities come into use, either in the state of ashes, or in a fermented state, as a valuable manure for green crops. Their value as manure is said to be enhanced in districts most removed from the sea; and this may not be merely on the principle that "cows afar off have long horns;" but the mineral substances they contain may be less abundant in the soils of inland districts than in those nearer the coast, to which the spray of the sea must carry a considerable quantity of these salts.

None of our common *Fuci* are known beyond the waters of the Atlantic except *F. vesiculosus*, which occurs in the Mediterranean Sea, and again in the Pacific, on the Western shore of North America. This species, indeed, is the most patient of the family in enduring a great variety of conditions. As to climate, it submits to the frozen rigour of the arctic circle, and to the tropical fervour of the Canary Islands. In the latter country, however, it appears to be on the very verge of extinction, the fronds being reduced to the smallest compass, consisting of little more than the root and the fructification; just as we see annuals grown in a poor and dry soil frequently dwindle to a pair of leaves and a flower, and these of the smallest size. Comparing the specimens from the Canary Islands with those grown in deep water in the north of Europe, we find so much difference, that they will hardly be suspected of being relations; yet the two forms may readily be traced into each other, and this without going beyond the evidence collected on our own shore. A change similar to that caused by heat in the plant from the Canaries is induced in this country by the very opposite conditions of fresh water and muddy soil. The *Fucus balticus* of northern writers, which is found in very muddy enclosed arms of the sea, near high-water-mark, and under the influence of fresh water, is a variety of *F. vesiculosus* much resembling, especially when in fruit, the starved variety found in the Canaries. This affords us a striking instance of the opposite means which Nature often employs to bring about the same result, and may teach us that the adaptations which we find in the various races of animals and plants have some other controlling cause than the circumstances in which the species find themselves. All we can determine on this subject seems to be, that every species of animal or plant has its natural condition, known only, in the first instance, to the Author of Nature; and that a departure from that natural condition, in either direction, will alter the character of the individual. But, until we have tested the matter by direct experiment, we cannot pronounce on the result. No one, by reasoning on the subject, would be prepared for the fact that the heat of the tropical sea would exercise the same transforming power on a particular plant as the mud and fresh water of a colder climate. A similar difference in the causes which effect the same end, may be noticed in comparing the means by which Nature provides a season of rest for the plants of tropical and of temperate climates. In temperate climates the cold and wet of autumn and winter strip the trees, and reduce the greater part of the vegetable kingdom to a state of torpor. Between the tropics * the same effect is brought about by the heat and drought of summer. The leaves of tropical trees (within certain parallels) are burned off the branches, while buds, coated with hard scales, are formed, that preserve the embryo foliage till the return of genial showers shall call forth the dormant powers of life. A tropical forest, so stripped, has much of the aspect of a wintry one in a temperate climate ; and, physiologically, the condition of vegetation is the same. But, what can be more opposite than the atmosphere—the light through which the pictures are seen ? The snow-clad earth, the clear and bracing air, and the dark-blue sky of a climate like that of Norway or Canada, contrast strongly with the burnt-up, dusty soil, air like the breath of a furnace, the hazy distance in which every object dances with a flickering motion, and the fierce heat that pours down from a pale blue sky. Yet the effect on vegetation is the same :—a season of rest is provided in either case, which is absolutely necessary to ensure the healthy growth of the plants of these opposite climates.

Close along the margin of the sea, either above or below high-water-mark, may be seen on most rocky shores, small circular somewhat scurfy patches, consisting of minute, rigid, branching plants. These, when dry, look perfectly black, but on the return of moisture

* See Gardner's " Travels in Brazil," p. 242, &c.

exhibit a clear olive-tint, while their tissues soften, and the frond becomes pliable. The patches I allude

LICHINA PYGMÆA AND CONFINIS.

to consist of two species or varieties of the genus *Lichina*; the smaller one, *L. Confinis*, growing just above high-water mark, where it is wetted by the spray without being submerged; the larger, *L. pygmæa*, growing in places inundated every tide. These little plants have sometimes been considered as *Algæ*, sometimes as belonging to the class of *Lichens*. By those who regard them as Algæ they are placed in the group of Melanosperms; but their fructification little resembles that of any of the genuine members of this group, while it has a considerable affinity to that of many Lichens. Most botanists now, therefore, consider them, as their first observers proposed, to belong to the true Lichens. Their submarine locality alone connects them with the Algæ. But submerged Lichens are by no means anomalous; several undoubted members of that family grow in places habitually flooded, such as the rocky beds of mountain rivulets, or even along the margin of the sea, within the range occupied by the *Lichinæ*.

About the limit of ordinary low-water, and to the depth of one or two fathoms beyond that limit, the rocky shore is fringed with a broad belt of luxuriant sea-plants, mostly consisting of the family called *Laminarieæ* —among which some of the larger members of the *Fucoideæ*, and a great number of the *Florideæ*, or Red

Sea-weeds, find a favourable locality. The *Laminarieæ* or Oar-weeds, are the largest of all sea-plants. Their stout, woody stems, and broad, ribbon-like, glossy, olive leaves, must be familiar to every one. When seen through clear water, as you pass over them in a boat, they form a picture resembling a miniature forest of palm-trees, as their great fronds stand expanded in the water, while fishes swim in and out among the flat branches. None of those of our climate attain a length of more than twelve or fourteen feet, and even at this size the weight of a single frond is very great. But, these are pigmies compared to some of the gigantic *Laminarieæ* of the Southern, Pacific, and Atlantic Oceans, where great trunks, twenty feet long and upwards, support huge bunches of leaves that form when expanded a circle of equal diameter. One species is said to have stems reaching to the enormous length of fifteen hundred feet, buoyed up by air-vessels from a great depth, and extending afterwards for a considerable distance along the surface of the sea. This plant, *Macrocystis pyrifera*, is found through most parts of the Pacific Ocean, and abounds in the southern parts of the Atlantic, but has not been noticed in the Northern Atlantic. Its stems are slender, becoming much branched, and bear a profusion of lanceolate, serrated leaves, each of which springs from an oblong air-vessel. Another species (*Nereocystis Lutkeanus*) from the north-west coast of America has stems, resembling whipcord, three hundred feet in length which support a great air-vessel at their extremities, six or seven feet long, crowned with a bunch of dichotomous leaves, each thirty or forty feet in length. On the air-vessels of this gigantic sea-weed, the Sea Otter, according to the observations of an excellent observer,* finds a favourite resting-place, when fishing; while the long, tenacious stems furnish the rude fishermen of the coast with excellent fishing-lines.

In tide-pools exposed to the sun, and also on the bottom of the sea beyond the tidal influence, the family of *Dictyoteæ* is found; generally scattered, but sometimes growing in society. These are the most beautiful members of the group of Melanosperms, and some of them, especially *Padina Pavonia*, or the Peacock's-tail, highly curious productions. This charming plant is only known with us on the south coast of England, where it occurs in many places; but it is one of the commonest shore-plants of the tropical sea, and also fringes the margin of the Mediterranean. It is an annual, appearing with the early summer, and fading before the autumn sets in. When growing, its fan-shaped fronds are rolled up into cups, while the delicate fibres with which they are bordered, and which form concentric bands over their surface, decompose the rays of light, and reflect the most beautiful glaucous and prismatic tints. The

PADINA PAVONIA.

* Dr. Henry Mertens, in Hook. Bot. Misc. vol. iii. p. 4, 5.

remainder of the Melanosperms, including the *Sphacelariæ* and *Ectocarpi*, are plants of small size, filamentous and much-branched, and form bunches or tufts, growing for the most part on other plants. Thus, most of the *Fuci* and *Laminarieæ* become covered, as the season advances, with small parasites belonging to these families:—and others grow on the smaller Algæ in tide-pools. Several are objects of much beauty.

With a short account of the Red Sea-weed or Rhodosperms I shall conclude this hasty sketch of the various tribes of Algæ. The Red Sea-weeds are by far the most numerous in species, the most beautiful in form and colour, and the most perfect or elaborate in structure of all the class of Algæ. They also characterise a greater depth of water. Many of them grow beyond the influence of the tide, and can only be procured by the dredge, except when a strong gale loosens them from their position, and throws them up on the beach. The majority grow close to low-water-mark, and are to be seen only for an hour or two at the spring-tides: so that a person visiting the shore at neap-tides may leave it ignorant of half its treasures. The favourite locality of the more delicate *Florideæ* (as the Rhodosperms are frequently called) is on the perpendicular sides of deep tide-pools under the shade of larger plants. In such places, either *Fucus serratus* or *Himanthalia lorea* commonly grows on the top of the rocky margin, while the fronds rest on the surface of the water. On removing the *Fuci* a host of delicately beautiful *Florideæ* will often be revealed. This is the usual position of the various species of *Griffithsia*, some of the most beautiful of the filiform Algæ. Where the pools

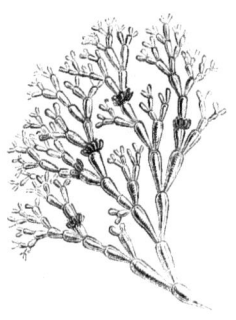

GRIFFITHSIA CORALLINA.

are not shaded by large plants on the margin, the northern aspect will be found most fertile, especially when ledges of rock project beyond the rest, and such is the favourite locality of *Delesserias anguinea*, whose beautiful rosy leaves, veined with darker striæ, are the delight of amateur collectors of sea-weeds.

Most *Floridèe* flourish in clear water. But this is not the case with several of the *Callithamnia*, the most delicate of the filiform kinds, whose slender pinnated fronds, when laid out on paper, resemble minutely beautiful tracery-work, and mock the attempts of the pencil to do them justice. The species of this genus flourish most in places where a coating of mud covers the rocks, or where the water itself is habitually muddy. Often the botanist, searching for *Callithamnia*, must content himself with bringing home handfuls of mud which merely exhibit the presence of some red filaments, till washed out: yet from this unpromising soil the most charming plants are often procured. A well-known and most successful collector of these plants, is in the habit of visiting, at low-water, in a boat, the muddy base of a small harbour-pier, and gathering indiscriminately any lump of red which the muddy surface of the pier affords:—and from the washings of these lumps,

Callithamnium gracillimum, C.thuyoideum, C.byssoideum and *Dasya ocellata,* and other rarities are procured. Mudbanks yield some of the most beautiful *Polysiphoniæ*, as for instance, *P. variegata;* but most of this genus prefer the purer water of rockpools. The exquisite *P. parasitica* is found only in clear water, at the verge of low tide or on the banks of Nullipores, which characterise a still lower level.

POL. PARASITICA.

I have spoken of the *Florideæ*, or Rhodosperms, as the Red Sea-weeds; but it must not be supposed that they are all of a clear red-colour,—nor does colour supply us with more than an imperfect guide in determining them. The red colour appears to depend in great degree on the amount of direct light which reaches the growing plant. The same species which exhibits a full red colour when growing in the shade, assumes every variety of paler tint till it ends in a clear yellow, as it grows under the influence of sunshine, and in shallower water. This is very apparent in the *Chondrus crispus*, or Carrigeen, well known for producing a peculiar gelatinous principle used in cookery and medicine. When this plant grows in places shaded from the sun, its fronds are of a very dark purple, reflecting prismatic colours from the surface: but growing, as it frequently does, in shallow pools exposed to full sunlight, it becomes green and even yellowish white before it altogether ceases to vegetate. Similar changes may be observed in many other common species, especially in *Ceranium rubrum*, and *Laurencia pinnatifida*. Light does not always act as a destroyer of colour among these plants—in some tribes it affects them by darkening the purples into browns, as in the *Polysiphoniæ*. Among these, *P. fastigiata*, which grows parasitically on *Fucus nodosus*, in places where it is exposed to the air for several hours every day, assumes the dark brown of a member of the olive-group. Mere colour, therefore, may lead the student into error, if he decide solely by it, to the neglect of peculiarities of structure and fructification.

Several of the Rhodosperms are in different countries either employed as articles of food or used in the arts, in the manufacture of strong sizes and glues. Their nourishing principle appears to reside in a peculiar compound found in several kinds, to which the name Carrigeenin has been given by the chemists. It was first extracted, as the name imports, from *Chondrus crispus*, the Carrigeen of our coasts, a plant which may be collected to an unlimited extent on all rocky parts of the British shores. The fronds, properly prepared by drying, will keep for any length of time, and a strong jelly may be extracted, when required, by simply boiling in water. Similar jellies are yielded by other species of *Chondrus*, as well as by the *Gigartinæ, Gracilariæ*, and certain *Gelidia*, some of which yield mucilages of so great strength as to be employed as glue. There have recently been imported into this country samples of an eastern species, *Gracilaria spinosa*, which, under the name *Agar-Agar*, is largely consumed in China, both as an article of food, and as yielding a very strong glue. The jelly prepared from it is certainly superior to that yielded by our *Chondrus*. A Swan River species (*Gigartina speciosa*, Sond.) affords a gelatine of perhaps equal value. Both these might be obtained in abundance, should a demand for them arise. These few instances, selected out of a multitude, show that the *Algæ* are not undeserving the notice of the economist, especially in a country where the constant increase of population renders desirable every effort to increase the supply of food. That the vast stores of Carrigeen which our coasts afford, have been wholly neglected during the recent famine, is the result partly of ignorance, and partly of the invariable companion of ignorance, —prejudice.

The only other Rhodosperms which I shall notice are the very curious tribe of *Corallineæ*,—the jointed Corallines of Linnæus,—plants which have been regarded, almost universally since the time of Ellis, as members of the animal kingdom. This tribe is most numerous in species as we approach the tropics, and the British examples are not many; but one of them, *Corallina officinalis*, is so common on all our coasts, that it must have attracted the notice of every one who has paid any attention to marine productions, and it will serve as a type of the family. It will at once be seen that this plant differs from other sea-weeds in being of a calcareous nature, effervescing when thrown into an acid solution; and in this respect it resembles a true coral. It neither produces Polypes, however, nor exhibits any animal character, while it yields spores, contained in receptacles perfectly analogous to those of the Algæ of the red series, to which its colour also allies it. These spores were observed and figured by Ellis; and it is therefore the more strange that the vegetable nature of the family has not been earlier acknowledged. *Corallina officinalis* generally occurs in society, covering the bottoms of shallow tide-pools with its jointed fronds, which afford a welcome resting-place to many of the smaller Algæ and to marine animals. It always springs from a broad, calcareous base, often of considerable thickness, which incrusts the surface of the rock. It commences to vegetate, though feebly, immediately within the limit of high-water, and extends throughout the whole littoral zone, gradually acquiring fuller developement as the water deepens; and the best specimens are always to be found nearest to low-water-mark. It is occasionally dredged from the depth of three or four fathoms, or perhaps more; but specimens from water of that depth are less perfect than those collected about low-water-mark, clearly showing that, at that level, the species is in the situation best adapted to its nature. The species of the genus *Corallina* are very imperfectly known, and many supposed species may ultimately prove to be merely varieties of this common and very generally diffused

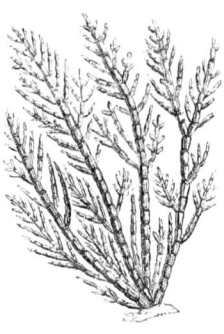
CORALLINA OFFICINALIS.

plant, which, in some form or other, inhabits the shores of most temperate latitudes.

Along with *Corallina officinalis*, and also creeping among the roots of various other Algæ, may often be seen the fronds of a lichenoid species of calcareous plant, *Melobesia* (or *Nullipora*) *lichenoides*, affixed to the surface of the rocky soil. This is of the same family as the *Corallina*, but simpler in structure. By some authors it is supposed to be merely the imperfectly developed state of a Coralline; but the evidence for this opinion does not appear satisfactory, and in the imperfect state of our knowledge it is better to consider these plants distinct. In appearance they are widely different, though similar in microscopic structure and substance. The *Melobesia* belongs to a group of the family, characteristic of a deeper water, and which we shall have occasion to speak of in our chapter on *Dredging*.

The very imperfect outline which I have just given of the several groups of marine plants, is all that the plan of this little volume admits of, without trenching too much on subjects of perhaps more general interest. The great elegance of many of the sea-weeds, and the ease with which specimens may be preserved, retaining much of their original beauty, attract many persons who occasionally visit the sea-shore ; and sea-weeds are collected either as objects of scientific interest, or for the manufacture of pictures for albums or screens. Those who collect sea-weeds for the latter purposes, in general care little to know their history; but perhaps when some of its facts are known, they may be regarded as not without interest. I have, therefore, mentioned some of the principles on which the classification of these plants is based, and described some of the commoner species of our shores. For a more detailed history of the family, I must refer my readers to books more expressly written on the subject.*

* See the Author's "Phycologia Britannica," containing coloured plates and detailed descriptions of all the British Sea-weeds: also, his "Manual of the British Marine Algæ," 2nd edit., with 27 plates of genera (*in preparation*).

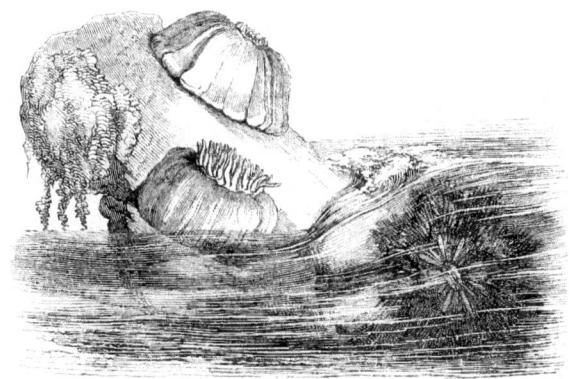

ACTINIÆ, OR SEA-ANEMONES.

CHAPTER IV.

THE ROCKY SEA-SHORE :—MARINE ANIMALS.

In the vegetation of the sea, nature has provided both shelter and food for an infinitude of animals. Were we to speak of the *uses* of sea-weeds, and confine ourselves to their adaptation to the wants of man, we should much misinterpret the office which this portion of the vegetable world discharges in the general economy. However great their uses to man, these are absolutely insignificant in comparison to those benefits for which the lower tribes of animated nature are indebted to the sea-weeds. Troop after troop of animals, one more highly organized than another, either derives its nourishment from the sea-weed itself, or uses the submarine forest as a hunting-ground, where it fulfils the appointed course of its busy life. Adhering to the roots of sea-weeds we find the scarcely organized, but obviously animated Sponge, whose place in the scale of creation seems so nearly balanced between the animal and the vegetable that naturalists have debated to which of the kingdoms it properly belongs. To the stems and leaves adhere multitudes of incrusting animals, some of which, till we examine them somewhat closely, and watch their animal motions and propensities with some care, seem to consist merely of masses of jelly; while others display, in their outward forms, the branching appearance of mosses, every branch clothed with scales, and crowned, when the animal is in vigour, with starry flowers. The rocks from which the sea-weeds spring afford a resting-place to stationary animals, which, in the shelter of these submerged groves, watch the approach of prey; and through the branches, in every direction, tribes as different from each other in form and structure as it is possible to conceive, sport and multiply, and contend in ceaseless motion. No spot of rock is absolutely desert, and no sea-weed grows that does not support its multitude of living things. The zoologist, therefore, on any rocky shore, may find abundant occupation; and he who does not limit himself to the mere collection and determination of new species, but enters into the more noble departments of his science — Anatomy and Physiology, — will in the most barren places find animals, the investigation of whose history will afford him constant sources of pleasure.

At the base of the animal scale, and apparently in close connection with the vegetable kingdom, yet when closely examined, resembling no vegetable in organization, is found the family of Sponges, a considerable number of which inhabits the shores of the British Islands. Dr. Johnston * enumerates fifty-six species, which he groups under nine genera, distinguished from one another by characters derived from differences in the structure and mineral composition of the skeleton. The outward forms of Sponges are exceedingly sportive, and even the same species, at different periods of its life, or under the influence of different circumstances, often exhibits an outward aspect of very opposite character. Some are, indeed, tolerably constant in form, especially the branching species ; but the majority are shapeless, or assume a form depending in great measure on the objects in connection with them. It thus becomes necessary, in studying the Sponges, to acquaint ourselves intimately with the exact structure of the skeleton. The spongy body is of the simplest nature ; it consists of a horny or sometimes stony network, composed of innumerable interlacing fibres, connected together and inosculating, till a porous mass, full of holes and passages, is the result. This is the skeleton, and such is seen in the common Sponges in everyday use. When the creature is alive, every portion of the horny fibre is coated over with a semifluid slimy matter, like a half-consistent jelly, seemingly inert and unorganized, and yet the seat of whatever life the Sponge contains. It is by this slime, which may be pressed out with the finger, that the network is depo-

* "History of the British Sponges and Corallines, by G. Johnston, M.D."

sited, and from it the whole growth of the mass proceeds. The slimy substance is apparently void of sensation, for it does not shrink when wounded; and the only motion resembling animal life which the mature Sponge exhibits is in the imbibition and expulsion of continuous currents of water. If any species of Sponge be examined, the holes with which the substance is everywhere pierced may be seen to be of two kinds, one of larger size than the rest, few in number, and opening into wide channels, or tunnels, which pierce the Sponge through its centre; the other minute, extremely numerous, covering the whole surface, and communicating with the innumerable branching passages which make up the body of the skeleton. According to the observations of Dr. Grant, water is freely imbibed through the smaller holes, and continuously expelled in jets through the larger, as long as the animal retains life. These currents may be seen if a small specimen of a living Sponge be placed in a watch-glass or other shallow vessel of salt-water, and examined through the microscope; and it appears to be through their agency that the substance is nourished. Nourishing particles dispersed through the water are received into the universal stomach, and what is not required is ejected through the canals.

Such is the simple history of the Sponges. Their propagation is provided for in a curious manner. At certain seasons of the year, if a Sponge be cut open, innumerable minute bud-like points will be found attached to the sides of the lining of the canals. These are the *gemmules* or young eggs of the sponge. As they increase in size they are gradually clothed with vibratile hairs (*cilia*); and at length, being fully formed, fall off as oval bodies; not inert, like the eggs of more active animals, or like their parents, but moving freely by the perpetual vibration maintained by their cilia. These cilia, by their united action, create strong currents round the little body, which drive it forward into the stream that issues from the opening of the Sponge, and thence into the open sea, where its motion is continued till it has reached a place suitable for its developement. When this is done it soon attaches itself; its wanderings cease, and it commences the quiet vegetative life of its parent. The instincts which guide animals in the care of their young are among the most interesting that the lower animals exhibit; but here, at the base of the scale, we find a passive parent whose young are endowed with powers of motion denied to its mature growth, and these obviously supply, by a beautiful arrangement, the deficiencies of the mother. When we look a little higher in the animal scale, we shall find other instances of greater activity in the young than in the mature animal; and even among the lower vegetable tribes, the spores are often endowed with proper movements. The little seed-like bodies from which the Algæ spring, are, in many instances, clothed with cilia, like the eggs of the Sponges, and enjoy, for a brief period, a similarly active life. The animal egg of the Sponge, and the vegetable egg of the *Conferva* are both moved by the same agency, and each appears to select the situation best adapted for its growth. The phases

EGG OF SPONGE.

of animal and vegetable existence have approached so near, that it requires the exercise of nicer tests than the eye to discriminate between them. We arrive at a point where the dry definitions of science cease to speak an intelligible language, and where the presence of the Unseen Worker begins to be felt.

In the history of the Sponges we find beings occupying nearly a middle rank between plants and animals, though necessarily considered as belonging to the latter. To such the term *Zoophytes*, or *animal plants*, might properly be given. This name is, however, commonly restricted by Naturalists to another group, clearly animal in their nature, but which exhibit a skeleton often branched like a plant, and bearing bodies resembling seed-vessels and flowers. I have incidentally alluded to these in a former chapter, and shall now enter into their history a little further. The rocky sea-shore will supply numerous species of this group of animals, from the fleshy Sea Anemone, the largest and most highly-organized of our native species, to the minute scaly *Lepralia*, which forms shagreened patches on the surface of rocks, shells, and sea-weeds. All the true Corals, including the precious coral of commerce and the Mushroom-Corals which ornament the cabinets of the curious, together with the horny, moss-like *Sertulariæ* of our own shores, are skeletons of the Zoophytes. The animals which inhabit them are termed Polypes, and are either single and solitary, as in the case of the Sea Anemone, or form a compound body, several individuals being connected together by a fleshy column, common to them all, through which a more or less perfect circulation is maintained, and unity given to the compound body. In so large a class we must expect to find great differences in organization; some are much simpler in structure than others; some are free to move about from place to place; others—and the greater number—are fixed, as by a root, to the surface of some object: but all the animals of the group have soft and inarticulate, bag-shaped bodies, furnished at the upper extremity with a mouth, or opening, leading to the stomach. The mouth is generally surrounded by one or more circles of fleshy arms, or *tentacula*, which expand, like the rays of a star, and in many cases are contractile, or capable, at the will of the animal, of being drawn in from their greatest extension, and transformed into mere fleshy, bud-like points. Tentacula, which, when fully expanded, are (in the *Hydra*) several inches in length, by a voluntary effort, and with great rapidity contract so as nearly to disappear altogether. In many kinds the tentacula, however, are non-contractile, and are either constantly expanded in the water, or merely drawn within the walls of the cell in which the animal lives, without any diminution of their volume. The Polypes possess no obvious nervous system. Their respiration is supposed to be conducted by cilia, which clothe the surface of the tentacula, and maintain a constantly changing current of water on the delicate surface of those organs.

While there is a great common resemblance between the skeletons, or polypidoms, of all the compound Zoophytes, the animals by whose organs they are secreted are so different, that zoologists arrange them in two classes,—the *Anthozoa*, which have a body capable of contraction in every part, and perfectly symmetrical, with but a single aperture for the entrance of food; and the *Polyzoa* (or *Bryozoa*), whose bodies are unsymmetrical, and incapable of contraction, while they are furnished with a separate mouth and vent. The first are obviously akin to radiate animals, while the latter show a close resemblance in structure to the simpler members of the Mollusca. The *Polyzoa*, though of much smaller size than many of the *Anthozoa*, are much more perfectly organized, and of a higher type in animal existence. In the compound *Anthozoa* the individuality of the Polypes is not clearly maintained, but each is, as it were, a bud issuing from a common fleshy trunk, of similar substance; while, in the *Polyzoa* every individual is distinct within its own precincts, though connected, like the Siamese twins, by a common band. Dr. Johnston aptly compares the former to "a chain of which all the links are welded;" the latter, "to a necklace, where the beads are strung together by a common thread." The *Anthozoa* are divided by Dr. Johnston into three orders, easily recognizable by the nature of their skeleton; the 1st, *Hydroida*, having Polypes enclosed in horny, tubular, plant-like sheaths, forming an external covering to their trunk; the 2nd, *Asteroida*, a calcareous or horny axis, or internal skeleton, surrounded by the fleshy parts of the compound body; and the 3rd, *Helianthoida*, having a calcareous or coriaceous skeleton composed of plates, radiating, like the gills of a mushroom, towards a common centre. The British *Asteroida* being all natives of the deeper parts of the sea, will more properly be noticed in the next chapter; I shall, therefore, here confine myself to a few common examples of the *Hydroida* and *Helianthoida*.

The old genera, *Tubularia* and *Sertularia* of Linnæus, now divided into many genera, furnish us with the best-known examples. We may take as an example of the first of these, a very common little species, found on stones and sea-weeds between tide-marks, especially in clear rock-pools. I allude to the *Coryne pusilla* of our present arrangement, to which name Dr. Johnston reduces five supposed species of authors. This little creature certainly varies much in size and degree of ramification;

CORYNE PUSILLA, AND MAGNIFIED PORTION.

but the differences are scarcely sufficient to separate permanent varieties. It offers us an instance of a very reduced skeleton, the tube being a thin, horny membrane, wrinkled cross-wise at very close intervals, and continued, in the shape of skin, over the terminal heads of the Polypes. The animal originates in creeping fibres. These throw up erect stems, from which are irregularly given off branches, each crowned with an oblong fleshy head, of a glassy lustre and red colour, armed with numerous short and thick tentacula, standing out like blunt spikes on every side, and but imperfectly retractile. The mouth is terminal. Though we call the club-shaped knob at the end of the branches a head, it in fact contains the whole proper body of the Polype, the substance which fills the tube being merely a medulla common to all. The flexibility of the branches, and their perfect union with the base of the head, enable the animal to move the latter part in every direction. Besides this, it can shorten or lengthen the head at pleasure, protruding the mouth, and bending it round to catch any object of prey. Its motions, which are slow, and not ungraceful in their deliberation, may readily be watched in a small vessel of sea-water, and specimens may be found on almost any rocky shore.

Of the restricted genus *Sertularia* seventeen British species are known, many of which are only found in deep water. I shall take as an example *S. filicula*, a common but elegant species, found on sea-weeds near low-water-mark, especially at the root of the larger Oar-weed, and often thrown up along the shore. The *Sertulariæ* are of a horny colour and texture, branched like plants, sometimes forked, but very generally feathered or pinnate. Their branches are toothed; and, when magnified, are found to consist of a single tube, jointed at intervals, and bearing along its sides prominent cells, alternate, or in opposite pairs, one placed at each side of the branch. In some species they are close together, and very distant in others. In these cells, which are hollow, and open at the end, the Polypes reside. When expanded, they show a mouth surrounded by several radiating tentacula; but they can withdraw themselves at pleasure within the narrow walls of their cell. Besides the cells in which the Polypes reside, most *Sertulariæ*,

produce bag-like bodies, called vesicles, in which their ova are contained. These are very rarely found on
S. filicula, but may be seen abundantly, especially in early spring, on another common species (S. operculata), which frequently forms a rigid beard to the stems of the great Oar-weed. The form of the vesicles varies much in different kinds, and often affords an excellent character to distinguish one closely-allied species from another. In *Plumularia cristata*, a beautiful feathery species,

SERTULARIA FILICULA, AND MAG. PORTION.

common on sea-weeds near low-water-mark, especially on *Halidrys siliquosa*, the vesicle is exceedingly curious, seemingly formed by the union and metamorphosis of several cells. It consists of an oblong pouch, with a tubular rib along its dorsal margin, from which issue numerous transverse, crested ribs, which will be better understood by the annexed figure than by a more detailed description. The genus *Plumularia* is readily known from *Sertularia* by having its cells unilateral, or all placed along one side only of the branches. Speaking of *Plumularia cristata*, Dr. Johnston introduces some reflections which apply equally to most of the Zoophytes of this division, and which I shall therefore quote. Each plume has been calculated to contain about five hundred Polypes, and a single specimen of ordinary size will number from five to six thousand. "Now," says Dr. Johnston, "many such specimens, all united, too, by

PLUMULARIA CRISTATA, AND MAGNIFIED VESICLE.

a common fibre, and all the offshoots of one common parent, are often located on one sea-weed, the site, then, of a population which nor London nor Pekin can rival. But *Pl. cristata* is a small species; and there are specimens of *Pl. falcata*, or *Sertularia argentea*, of which the family may consist of eighty to one hundred thousand individuals. It is such calculations, always underrated, that illustrate the 'magnalities of Nature,' and take us by surprise, leaving us in wonderment at what may be the great object of this her exuberant production of these 'insect millions peopling every wave.'" * But,

> So He ordained, whose way is in the sea,
> His path amidst great waters, and His steps
> Unknown ;—whose judgments are a mighty deep,
> Where plummet of Archangel's intellect
> Could never yet find soundings ; but from age
> To age let down, drawn up, then thrown again
> With lengthened line and added weight, still fails ;
> And still the cry in Heaven is, ' O the depth ! '
>   MONTGOMERY.

---

* Johnston's Brit. Zoop. p. 93.

Such are the characters of some of our commoner compound Zoophytes. We shall next examine a few belonging to the order *Helianthoida,* which are of a very different description, being solitary or simple Polypes. The commonest and best known of these are the Sea Anemones or *Actiniæ,* several kinds of which are to be found on every shore. When the Sea Anemone is left dry by the retiring tide, it withdraws its tentacles from view by retracting them within the mouth, and the whole body shrinks into a conical lump of wrinkled flesh. The same happens if the creature be touched with a finger while expanded. Were we to form our idea of its beauty by inspecting it in this state, we should have little cause to stop and admire it. But, placed in water, and allowed to recover itself, few marine animals are more beautiful than the various kinds of these *Actiniæ.* They may aptly be compared to the flowers of Mesembryanthema, with their myriads of lustrous petals forming a starry whole. Here the tentacula, which surround the disc in many rows, represent the petals of the flower, or may be likened to the "rays of glory" in the passion-flower; and, in the brilliancy of their colours, and the lustre of their substance, they much exceed their vegetable analogues. It is impossible, in an uncoloured woodcut, to do justice to creatures displaying sometimes the most delicate, sometimes the richest tints, but the vignette at the head of this chapter may serve to give some general notion of their contour to persons who have never seen them. Those who visit the rocky sea-shore will soon recognise in the deep tide-pools near low-water-mark numerous beautiful kinds, ornamented with all the colours of the rainbow.

The internal structure of the Sea Anemone is very curious. The Polypes of the *Hydroida* are exceedingly simple in structure, their flesh being composed of a homogeneous mass of cells, heaped together, and formed into a bag-like body. In these *Helianthoida* the structure is much more compound : there is an outer leathery skin, separated from the inner coat or wall of the stomach by a hollow space, in which are placed numerous vertical partitions or laminæ, radiating towards the centre like the gills of a mushroom. These plates have their origin on the inner surface of the leathery coat, to which they act as a support ; some of them project so far as to touch the walls of the stomach, and others are narrower and shorter than the rest, exactly as we find the gills of a mushroom. A similar structure is found represented in stone, in the well-known Mushroom Coral or Madrepore of our cabinets, which is indeed the skeleton of an animal closely allied to the Sea Anemone. In the Sea Anemone, the laminæ continue fleshy during the life of the animal ; in the Madrepore they secrete a coating of carbonate of lime, which thickens by degrees, and at length forms a stony cast of the animal. The lower parts gradually die away, as the stony matter increases, while the Polype-body, continuing to live, is pushed upwards, and thus the Corals of this family are produced. In the seas of tropical and subtropical countries, the species of Calcareous Corals of the *Helianthoid* order are exceedingly numerous, and their office in the natural economy most wonderful. Ceaselessly, from the earliest ages of the world, have they gone on, withdrawing lime from the waters of the sea, and fixing it in their tissues, till not mountains or islands merely, but whole continents have been formed by their *débris*. In the limestones of many districts vast beds of fossil Madrepores are found. The well-known ornaments manufactured at Torquay, exhibit beautiful sections of antediluvian animals of this group. The work is still in progress. Fresh beds of such limestones, of unknown extent, are gradually forming throughout the Pacific Ocean, and along the shores of the great southern continent of New Holland. In our British seas, very few examples of this section of Zoophytes remain, of the multitudes which once inhabited our shores; but in the modern sea one does exist, to which a considerable geological interest is attached, from its being also undoubtedly found in the crag formation. This Coral, *Turbinolia Milletiana*, has been dredged in a living state off the coast of Cornwall, and off the west of Ireland ; but it is very rarely found. A more common species, *Caryophyllea Smithii*, is found on various parts of the coast. It bears a miniature resemblance to the exotic Madrepores, having the same mushroom folds ; while its animal, when expanded, closely resembles a common Sea Anemone.

CARYOPHYLLEA SMITHII.

Twenty different kinds of *Actiniæ*, or Sea Anemones, are known to British Naturalists, but probably several others remain unnoticed. Many have as yet been seen in only one locality; the history of others is very imperfectly known; and accurate drawings of several kinds are wanting: there is, therefore, still open a most interesting field to the observer of these beautiful creatures. Among their allies is a particularly elegant species, often found adhering to the smaller sea-weeds in rock-pools. With the general aspect of an *Actinia*, it differs in having a bell-shaped body, raised on a narrow stalk, and in having its tentacula collected in tufts at regular distances round the margin. These differences are sufficient to mark a generic group, which is called *Lucernaria*, and of which three species have been found on the British coast. The most common is distinguished by having a marginal tubercle in the centre of the space between each tuft of tentacles.

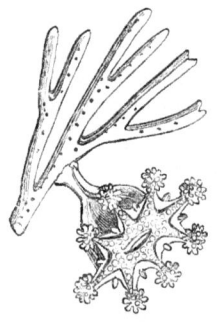

LUCERNARIA AURICULA.

Its body is clear as crystal, and coloured variously in different specimens, being sometimes green, sometimes red, and sporting into various other tints. When it desires to shift its quarters, it can detach itself at will from the object to which it adheres, and swim, with considerable quickness, to a new position, by alternately expanding and contracting its body.

All the Polypes we have yet spoken of, belong to the class *Anthozoa;* but we must remember that there is another class of these creatures, with an organization quite different, though with an outward similarity in the polypidom, namely, the *Polyzoa*, or, as they are as commonly called, the *Bryozoa*, or Sea Mosses. In the *Anthozoa*, the skeleton, whether horny or stony, has little or no organic connection with the fleshy parts, to which it acts as an internal support, or an external defence; for though secreted by the organs of the Zoophytes, when it is once formed, it has no further capability of developement, and no circulation is maintained through its substance. But in the *Polyzoa* the polypidom continues to be, at all times, a living portion of the animal which inhabits it. It is, in fact, a sort of hardened skin, closely adhering to the Polype, and continuous with its softer parts. None of the animals of this group occur in a naked or separate form. They are all associated in compound bodies, and lodged in cells, within which, when at rest, the Polype lies concealed, doubled up upon itself. They do not possess the remarkable contractile powers of the *Anthozoa*, but when they retreat within their cells, they merely fold themselves closely together. When expanded, the fore-part of the body is protruded, exhibiting a mouth surrounded by a circle of slender tentacula. The species of this class are very numerous, but mostly of smaller size and less beauty than those of the *Anthozoa*. A considerable number are merely scaly crusts, adhering to the surface of rocks and Algæ. These, when carefully examined, exhibit the beauty and regularity of structure inseparable from the works of creation, but are commonly passed over by the collectors of pretty things, as merely white, scaly crusts, altogether devoid of interest. What the parasitic fungi are to larger vegetables, these little animals are to their more showy neighbours. But even in the humblest kinds, it is astonishing what a variety of beautiful structures are met with. The common observer may pass over the species of *Lepraliæ* without discrimination, as being merely rude scurfs, deforming the sea-weeds or shells over which they spread ; but, if

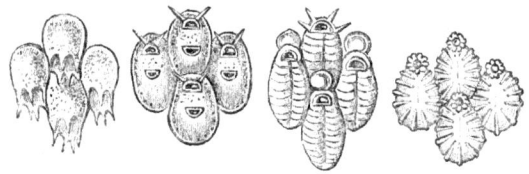

VARIOUS SPECIES OF LEPRALIÆ, MAGNIFIED.

he carefully examine them, nearly forty kinds, distinguished by very curious and elegant varieties of form, will reward his labour. The polypidom in this genus consists of a single layer of cells, adhering by their under surface to rocks, shells, or sea-weeds, and disposed in regular order in a more or less perfectly circular manner, formed row beyond row, in concentric layers. Some of the more curious forms of the cells are represented magnified in our figure.

Several of the *Polyzoa*, especially those of the family called *Escharidæ*, have appendages to their cells of a very singular nature, the use of which has not yet been determined. These odd-looking organs are attached to the outer side of the cell, and resemble in form the head of a bird furnished with a bill which can open and shut like a pair of pincers. Each head is fixed on a flexible stalk, and while the creature lives, maintains a constant and regular motion up and down, opening and shutting the bill at intervals. All specimens of the same species do not produce them, nor are they found on all the cells of a single specimen; and they exist indiscriminately on certain species of different genera, while often species, otherwise closely allied, are not furnished with them.

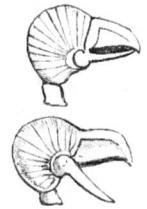

APPENDAGE OF CELLULARIA.

From this group of the class Zoophytes we pass, by a very easy transition, to the more simple members of the MOLLUSCA, those forming the subdivision *tunicata*. They are so called, because their soft parts are enclosed, not in a shell, like the majority of the class, but in a tough, leathery coat or tunic. The commonest example of a tunicated Mollusc is found in the various kinds of *Ascidiæ*, or Sea Squirts, some of which are found attached to sea-weeds and stones, in the littoral zone; others are frequently thrown up from deeper water on the beach, and may be dredged in abundance in almost any locality. Some are of a large size, several inches in length. Their outer form is that of a bag, with a smooth or variously-roughened semi-transparent skin, furnished with two small openings, through which, on the slightest pressure, a jet of water is sent to a considerable distance. These creatures lead a very inactive life. Attached by their base to plants, they trust for nourishment to whatever small fry are brought to their mouths by currents in the water. They have not the elegance of form of the Sea Anemones, but many are painted with the most gaudy colours. Their internal structure is very simple, and connects them closely with the division of Mollusca which form bivalve shells,—the tunic in the *Ascidiæ* being strictly analogous to the shell of the Conchifer. Their metamorphoses have been watched by several distinguished Naturalists, and offer highly curious points in their history. In the young or tadpole state, they are extremely active, swimming about by rapid motions of their tail, till the young creature finds a spot where he can take root. Then the tail disappears, and grasping fibres, or roots, spring from the body, which gradually assumes the form, and adopts th quiet life of the parent from which it sprung. It is thus, by giving to the young animal powers which she denies to the fully grown, that Nature, in these and many other of the stationary lower animals, provides for the proper dispersion of the species. Among more perfect animals, it is the old take care of the young, and provide for them: here we find the young possess instincts which they lose at an advanced period of their life.

The *Ascidiæ*, which, because they are common and of large size, I have instanced as examples of the tunicated Mollusca, are simple animals, each creature living by itself; but I should give an imperfect idea of the class if I did not allude to the compound Ascidians, animals of similar structure, which yet live associated, or connected together into a compound body, such as we have already seen among the Zoophytes. These are very numerous on our shores; but the most varied forms are taken only by the dredge. Still, on the stems of Sea-weeds, within tide-marks, especially on the various kinds of *Cystoseira*, and on the *Laminariæ*, numerous kinds, some of them extremely beautiful, may be found. The stems of the Olive-coloured Sea-weeds are often literally concealed, by clasping masses of firm jelly, whose surface is marked with radiating stars, blue, crimson, or orange,—or various in colour, resembling a tesselated pavement, or the polished section of a Torquay madrepore-stone. These belong to the animals in question, and to the tribe *Botryllidæ*. The gelatinous crust is a matrix common to the whole community; while each star that glitters on its surface, consists of numerous separate individuals, similar in most points of their structure to the bag-like *Ascidiæ*. It is impossible, without colour, to do justice to such delicate creatures by a figure, and the wood-cut in the margin is merely intended to guide the eye. A brief outline of what is known of the British species of this highly curious family, is given in the first chapters of Forbes' and Hanley's "British Mollusca," to which I must refer for further information: but a more complete history, accompanied by coloured figures, is required before the study of these curious creatures can be rendered popular.

BOTRYLLUS.

These Ascidians are among the humblest members of the great class of MOLLUSCA. This class includes the whole group of animals which produce what are properly called shells, the favourite study of the conchologist; also a multitude which are shell-less at all periods of their life; and others, whose shells are reduced to membranous plates concealed under the fleshy folds of their bodies. Commencing with the shapeless bag of the *Ascidiæ*; proceeding thence, through the bivalve shells into Sea Slugs; and so, through the various tribes of univalve shells,—we pass under review a great variety of animals, rising in complication of structure one above another, until we arrive at the Nautilus and the Cuttlefish, which close the great group, by a type of structure in which the peculiar organization of the vertebrate is dimly sketched. The lowest Mollusca are scarcely more organized than the Zoophytes: the highest closely border on the most perfect animals. The study of this class therefore is, in all respects, highly important. To the mere student of comparative anatomy it offers a rich field of research; for here, within circumscribed bounds, he can trace the gradual developement of organs from the first idea, as it were, to their full perfection. To the collector of beautiful objects, the countless varieties of shells, so easily preserved and so varied in contour and colour, afford continual sources of interest; and their proper classification, a pleasant problem for the exercise of ingenuity:—although it must be admitted that the proper classification of shells cannot be arrived at, if the nature of the animal which forms them be not carefully studied. A striking proof of this is shown in the genus *Patella*, of the older authors. If we merely consider the form of the shell, this group appears to be strictly natural. But when we examine the creatures of which these shells are the covering, we find them so differently organized that it is impossible to regard them as of the same genus. It would therefore be just as natural, classing quadrupeds by their skins, to place the leopard and the camelopard in the same genus because they have similar coats, as it would be to combine, under one group, the various species of the Linnæan genus *Patella*. Conchology, within a few years, has made more advances in a philosophical direction than most of the other natural sciences. Up to a recent period, it was the lowest of all scientific pursuits, and appeared the most useless. Now, however, that the subject begins to be studied on better principles, a new light has burst upon it, and a thousand interesting facts in the lives of the shell-coated animals, are revealed.

Nor is the interest which attaches to Conchology merely derived from our increased knowledge of the habits and instincts of an extensive class of animals. Its bearings on Geology place it among the most important of the minor divisions of Zoology. Shelly-coated Mollusca have existed in the waters of the sea and of rivers from a very early period of the world's history, and have left in most stratified rocks and gravels abundance of their shells, preserved in a more perfect manner than the remains of most other animals. Now, as the species in the early rocks differ from those found in later formations, quite as much as the latter from the Mollusca of our modern seas, the gradual change in the character of the imbedded shells marks a certain interval of time in the world's history. To understand and apply the evidence derivable from this source, requires a most careful study, not only of the different forms of fossil-shells, but of the forms and habits of existing species. In fact, it is impossible to understand the character of these fossils without an intimate knowledge of Conchology. To distinguish species,—to insist on minute characters,—to collect minute shells,—appear often to the unthinking utilitarian but trifling hobbies of mere triflers. Yet on these apparent trifles depend some of the most important problems of Geology; and if the conchologist blunder in reading the "Medal of Creation,"* all the deductions of the geologist will be vitiated. To trace the history of a species of shell, from its first appearance in an early bed, to its final extinction in a later formation, requires an intimate knowledge, not merely of the species in question, but of the changes which, under modified circumstances, other species undergo, before their vitality yields to an altered condition. It is a highly curious fact, that there is a term to the life of a species, as well as to that of an individual. What that term is we know not; but the remains of extinct species and genera prove the fact. But before the final extinction of a species,—except the change of circumstances be so sudden as to cause the instantaneous death of every individual of the kind,—the fry developed under altered circumstances of habitat will vary from the characters of their parents, and present the peculiarities of the species in a weakened degree; their

* I need scarcely remind the reader that there is such a book as Dr. Mantell's "Medals of Creation."

DECLINE OF SPECIES. 103

descendants, if they have any, will be of still feebler character; and, should the modifying cause continue to increase, the species will then probably cease to exist. The sudden and complete influx of fresh water to a basin previously covered by the sea would instantaneously kill all its testaceous animals. But were the change gradual, these same animals and their descendants would exist in water considerably less salt; though they would probably cease to propagate before the lake had become wholly fresh. A curious instance of gradual change in a fossil marine species from the influx of fresh water, was observed by Professor E. Forbes* in the island of Cos. In this case the change of circumstance was clearly marked, through the several beds in which the shell occurred, till the species altogether ceased. These forms or varieties, depending on the influx of fresh water are shown in the annexed figure. I have noticed similar change in the character

SHELL FROM LYCIA, E. F.

of the common *Littorina rudis* of our own coasts, whose shell, when the animal occupies its proper habitat, between tide-marks, is thick and strong, with shallow grooves between the spires. But this species sometimes climbs up rocks of considerable height, and remains upon them, trusting to the washing of the spray for its nourishment. The specimens I allude to were found among the crevices of a sea-cliff on the West of Ireland,

* "Travels in Lycia," 2 vols. 8vo., 1847.

at a height of nearly two hundred feet above the sea, a situation which the tide never washes over, but where the giant waves of the Atlantic throw up pretty constantly a feathery spray. This spray collects in pools on the summit of the crag, where it is largely diluted with rain-water; and here, in this unpromising locality, multitudes of *Littorina rudis* have taken up their abode. The specimens are quite as large as the usual state of the species, but the substance of the shell is nearly as thin as that of a *Limneus*, especially about the aperture, and the grooves between the spires are much deeper than usual. Still, though changed, the species is easily recognized;—nor is there the slightest disposition to pass into *L. petræa.*

I have already, in the chapter on *Sands*, spoken of some of the general habits and structure of the *bivalve* Mollusca, the great majority of which live in sandy or muddy places. Some, however, like the *Edomites*, take up their abode in the rock, and hollow out for themselves dwellings in it. Such is the *Pholas*, of which we have several British species, which are often found imbedded in limestone or sandstone rock, though occasionally they content themselves with houses of clay. How so frail a shell as *Pholas candida*, which is as thin as paper, and as brittle as glass, is

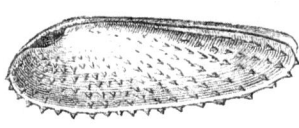

PHOLAS CANDIDA.

able to work its way through hard stone, has long been a puzzle to Naturalists; some of whom assert that it works by means of an acid solvent; others that it bores like an auger, by revolving, and rasps away the surface of the rock with the rough points on its surface. The question remains a knotty one, and my space forbids me to discuss it here. The *Mussels* are another group of bivalve shells, which inhabit rocky ground, but are incapable of burrowing into the rock. Nature has not, however, left them unprovided with means for securing their position. She has destined them to a sedentary life on the naked surface of rocks, exposed to the greatest violence of the waves. The common *Mytilus rugosus*, or Rock Mussel, may be seen covering, by thousands, the surface of rocks near low-water-mark, always choosing the most open situations. But here it is as firmly anchored as a ship in harbour. Its foot, which is so small as to be useless for purposes of progression, is employed in weaving silken threads of great strength, which it affixes to the rock and to its neighbour mussel; and thus mutually combined, and each grasping the rock, the community of mussels live together in security.

But the great majority of the Mollusca which inhabit rocky places belong to a very extensive group, called *Gasteropoda*, the whole of the under side of whose body consists of a strongly muscular, flattened foot, on which they glide along with a slow but regular motion, leaving generally a slimy track behind them. It is needless to say that the Slug and the Snail are examples of a naked and a shell-covered Mollusc of this kind. But not merely these land Molluscs, but all the univalve marine and fresh-water shells, and all the naked Sea

106   GASTEROPODOUS MOLLUSCA.

Slugs, properly so called, belong to this class of *Gasteropoda.* There is here an obvious advance in organization above the bivalves, even in the external characters of the animal. The body is more symmetrical; there is a greater distinction of parts,—an obvious head, an evident tail; and, save that the body is without legs, we have often a considerable outward resemblance to some vertebrate animal, in the form of the body and in the expression of the countenance. For here is a well-formed face, surmounted by two or four tentacula, commonly called horns, which either, as in the Snail, carry each an eye at its summit, or, as is the case in most of the marine kinds, have an eye on a prominence at the base. When we look at the internal structure of these animals, the advance in organization is still more clearly shown. The organs of digestion and of circulation are formed on a very perfect type, and the nervous system is not only amply developed, but there is a well-defined nervous centre, or brain. The mouth, in many species, is furnished with sharp and strong teeth; in others, the process of digestion is facilitated by strong, bony gizzards, which bruise the food in its

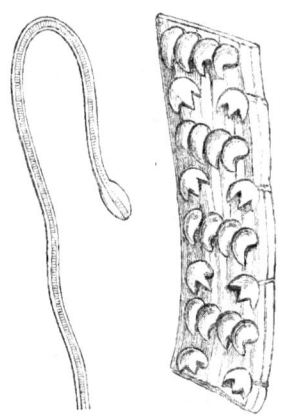
LIMPET'S TONGUE.

passage into the stomach; and in others the tongue is armed with spinous processes, obviously intended to assist in the preparation of the food. The tongue of the Common Limpet, shown in the preceding figure, is a curious piece of mechanism. It is from two to three inches long, and half a line in diameter, flat, between horny and membranous, with a spoonlike extremity, and when at rest, retracted into the stomach. Its whole extent is armed with transverse rows of sharp, hooked teeth, four in each row; and between the rows, are placed two trifid, rather obliquely-set teeth, one at each side of the strap. Our figure shows the general form of the whole tongue, and a small portion magnified.

So large a class as the *Gasteropoda* necessarily includes animals of very different aspect and variously modified structure, which it becomes necessary to classify on some principle derived from their organization. The classification usually adopted is founded on differences in the shape and position of the gills, or breathing apparatus. The Common Land Snail, as well as the Fresh-water Snails, breathe air, which is received into a cavity lined with a delicate network, analogous to the lungs of air-breathing animals; and the fresh-water kinds are obliged to rise to the surface every time they require to take in fresh air. These constitute the first group, or *Pulmoni branchiata*. Such a mode of aërating the blood would obviously be unsuited to marine *Gasteropoda*; consequently, all the remaining orders are furnished with gills, variously placed. There are eight of these orders; and I shall mention five, as containing animals commonly met with. The *Nudibranchiata*,* or Slugs with naked gills, have the gills placed on the outside of the body, expanding freely in the water, like the tentacula of the Sea Anemone. Few marine animals offer more beautiful forms, gaily ornamented with colours, and fringed with tentacula; while their breathing apparatus often displays the most elaborately-branched leaves, placed like the petals of a flower. The *Tectibranchiata*, or Slugs with covered gills, are animals of a something similar aspect, apparently soft Slugs, but often furnished with an internal shell. In these the gills are placed on one side of the body, under the deep folds of the mantle. Among seaweeds, near low-water-mark, a deep purple Mollusc of this group may be found, called *Aplysia*. It is one or two inches long, with a snail-like body, a prominent head, furnished with four ear-shaped tentacula, two near the tip of the snout, and on the forehead two more, at the base of which are seen a pair of small, peering

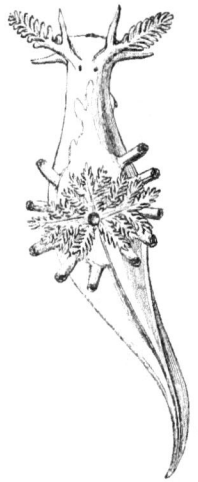

ANCULA CRISTATA.

* A monograph of the British species of this group, illustrated by exquisitely beautiful plates, is in course of publication (through the Ray Society) by Messrs. Alder and Hancock.

eyes. The back of the creature opens with two wide lobes, which can be expanded or closed over the opening at the animal's will. When open, they expose to view, on the right side, the finely fringed and lobed branchiæ, seated in a deep hollow beneath a fold of the mantle.

Next stand the *Pectinibranchiata*, the most numerous order of *Gasteropods*, comprising all the spiral univalve shells. In these the gills are pectinated, or shaped like the teeth of a comb, and placed in a large hollow chamber in the animal, communicating with the surface by a wide slit, through which the water finds free access to the gills. This type is obviously analogous to the Pulmoniferous order, except that in these the medium is water, and not air. Closely allied to this order are the *Scutibranchiata*, which have pectinated gills, similarly placed in a special chamber; but in these the shell is wide, and cup- or shield-shaped, instead of being spiral. Such is the Common Limpet (*Patella*), which may be taken as the type of the order. And, lastly, I shall mention the *Cyclobranchiata*, in which the gills form a fringe round the margin of the body, between the edge of the mantle

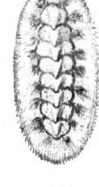

CHITON MARGINATUS.   CHITON FASCICULARIS.

and the foot. To this belongs the *Chiton*, the only multivalve shell among the *Gasteropoda*. There are two or three common species, which may be found adhering to stones near low-water-mark. They are Slugs, coated with eight transverse, shelly plates, resembling the plates of ancient armour, which, connected with a tough marginal band, form a complete shield to the animal.

These several orders of *Gasteropoda* are as various in their habits as in their organization. A large number feed on marine plants, but many are carnivorous, preying on other Mollusca, as well as on any animal substance offered to them. Among spiral shells, those with circular mouths to the shell, like the old genus *Turbo*, are vegetable feeders; while such as have an aperture ending in a canal, like *Buccinum* and *Murex*, are animal-feeders. Very important modifications of internal structure indicate this difference of food, and the external organs, particularly about the mouth, exhibit a corresponding variety of form. In those which feed on vegetables the mouth is generally a slit, furnished with more or less perfect lips, armed with a simple cutting apparatus, which is often a powerful instrument, enabling the animal to eat its way through comparatively hard substances. But the animal feeders are provided with a much more complex organ, which serves the double purpose of an arm to secure the prey, and a channel to convey it to the stomach. The proboscis of the Whelk, or *Buccinum*, is an organ of this character of a highly curious structure; and, armed with it, the creature can pierce through the hardest shells in search of food. This proboscis can either be protruded to a considerable length, and used as an arm moveable in every direction, or it may be wholly drawn in, contracting on itself, like the horns of a snail, till it disappear within the body of the animal. Its movements depend on the action of a very complex system of muscles. It consists of two cylinders, one within the other; the outer of which serves for the attachment of the motor muscles and the general protection of the organ, while the inner, opening near the extremity with a longitudinal mouth, armed with two strong cartilaginous lips, encloses the tongue and a great part of the œsophagus. The tongue is armed with sharp spines, and, acting in concert with the hard lips, which can be opened or shut, or strongly pressed together, it forms a sort of rasp or auger, by which very hard substances are rapidly perforated; and then the tongue being protruded, the hooked spines with which it is armed are admirably fitted for the collection of food. The mode in which the shells of *Gasteropoda* are formed is very similar to what takes place among bivalve shells. These beautifully painted structures are secreted by the glandular margin of the mantle, or soft skin, which clothes the upper part of the body of the Mollusc; and their form depends on the shape of the body they are destined to cover, while the outline of the border is alike regulated by that of the mantle. In the border of the mantle are placed the glands through which colouring-matter is added to the lime of which the shell consists, and here also the whole of the outer coat of the shell is formed by constant annual additions to the lip. The after-growth of the shell in thickness, is provided for by secretions almost always colourless, from the general surface of the mantle. These are supplied in thin layers, one over the other, at stated periods, so that the older a shell is, the thicker will be the substance. In most of the shell-coated *Gasteropods* the mantle is concealed by the shell, or its margin only may be seen just protruded round the aperture, as the creature crawls along; but in the *Cypræa*, or Cowry, and in such shells as have a similarly polished coat, the mantle folds back over the surface of the shell, to which it imparts the high polish and the beautiful markings

NASSA RETICULATA.

these shells display. The annexed section of the shell of *Nassa reticulata* is intended to show the nature of its internal spires.

Notwithstanding the defences provided by Nature for the shelly Molluscs, they have many enemies, from whose attacks the largest and strongest shells do not always afford protection. Among these enemies are some animals which have no means of piercing the shell, but must watch their opportunity when the owner is quietly feeding, or so far extended that he cannot retreat before the fatal blow is given. No one can have picked up many spiral shells on the shore without noticing that several of them were tenanted, not by the proper owner of the shell, but by a kind of Crab, which has taken up his abode in "the hollow-wreathed chamber." These Crabs belong to a peculiar genus, called *Pagurus*, or the Hermit Crabs, which are obviously fitted by Nature for such a life, and unsuited to any other; and the *Pagurus* would find himself quite as much inconvenienced by the loss of his stolen coat as the natural owner himself. We may, therefore, wonder that Nature should have left him so unprovided as to subject him to the necessity of feloniously appropriating the goods of another. But, it may well be replied, that he was specially destined to keep the shelly Molluscs in check, as some enemies seem provided to every animal, that the balance might be preserved between the several species of the animal kingdom. But, be this as it may, we find in the formation of the *Pagurus* his charter for acting as he does. All the forepart of his body is coated with mail, like that of other crabs, while his hind-parts are soft, and covered with a membrane in which the mere rudiments of shelly plates may be traced. The tail, however, is furnished with a pair of hooks, by which it can lay hold of objects. The back part of his body, indeed, so obviously resembles that of one of the Spiral-shelled Molluscs, that it requires but a glance to see that the cast-off clothes of one will equally suit the other. And in early life the *Paguri* are probably contented with nestling in the deserted shells which may be found on the shore, and to which they readily attach themselves by means of the hooks of their tail, so that they can move about with as great ease as if there was a regular organic adhesion. But, as they advance in size, they require larger houses; the first-selected shells are therefore deserted, and new ones chosen. Sometimes the *Pagurus* continues to select deserted shells. But, judging from the freshness of the shell in which we find him, it is probable that he more frequently attacks living specimens, seizing the animal with his claws before it has time to retreat; and, having devoured its flesh, appropriates the shell. Mr. Bell* states that such is probably the fact, though he has not himself witnessed it.

* "History of British Crustacea," p. 173.

It would extend this chapter too much to mention, or even to glance at, the other groups of animals, examples of which are to be found on the rocky sea-shore. Enough has been said to show the richness of the subject. No shore is so absolutely barren but it will provide some interesting object for investigation among the lower animals, and there will generally be found everywhere examples of all the greater groups. And there are few shores which produce nothing but common kinds; the most unfavourable-looking places often unexpectedly yield something which is rarely found. The pursuit of Marine Zoology is, therefore, always interesting, for the attention is kept constantly alive. With the varying nature of the ground the population varies. And nothing can well exceed the beauty of a clear rock-pool, seen under strong sunlight, and through a calm surface, tenanted by its varied animated tribes, all fulfilling the duties allotted to their several kinds. The transparent shrimp, now resting on its oars, midway in the water, watching your motions with its peering eyes, and attentive to the slightest disturbance, now darting through the pool, and hiding himself among sea-weeds; the basking Sea Anemone displaying his starry flowers; the Purple Rock Urchin* studding the bottom of the pool with spiny globes; and the quiet Molluscs leisurely pursuing their way, feeding as they go: these, mingled

---

* This species, *Echinus lividus*, is peculiar to the west coast of Ireland, where it is very common, living in society in pools between tide-marks. Its habits are as curious as its aspect is beautiful. It is chiefly remarkable for burrowing circular holes in limestone, clay-slate, or even in trap-rocks.

with the varied contour and colour of delicate sea-plants, form a picture which has its prototype nowhere but in fairy-land.

> "The sounds and seas, each creek and bay,
> With fry innumerable swarm, and shoals
> Of fish that with their fins, and shining scales,
> Glide under the green wave, in sculls that oft
> Bank the mid sea: part single, or with mate,
> Graze the sea-weed their pasture, and through groves
> Of coral stray; or sporting with quick glance,
> Show to the sun their waved coats dropped with gold;
> Or, in their pearly shells at ease, attend
> Moist nutriment; or under rocks their food
> In jointed armour watch: on smooth the seal
> And bended dolphins play: part huge of bulk,
> Wallowing unwieldy, enormous in their gait,
> Tempest the ocean: there leviathan,
> Hugest of living creatures, on the deep,
> Stretched like a promontory, sleeps or swims.
> And seems a moving land; and at his gills
> Draws in, and at his trunk spouts out, a sea."
>
> MILTON.

NATURALISTS USING THE DREDGE.

CHAPTER V.

DREDGING.

AMONG the amusements of the sea-shore there is, perhaps, none so capable of yielding a varied pleasure to a person whose taste for Natural History is awakened, as dredging, where it can be carried on under favourable circumstances. It is not on every coast that dredging can be practised. On some, the surf is habitually too great to admit of boating, as on parts of the west of Ireland, where a rock-bound shore presents no harbours for boats, and the fishermen are destitute of any other than canvas canoes, totally unfit for the purposes of dredging. On these coasts the broad waves of the Atlantic, continually rolling in, keep up a troubled water, in which the pursuits of the deep-sea naturalist can rarely be carried on. In other places, a rocky, or as it is technically called a foul, bottom, presents insuperable obstacles to the use of a dredge. It is only, therefore, in certain favoured localities that dredging can be resorted to as an amusement by the frequenter of the sea-shore. Land-locked bays and harbours, where a quiet water flows over a smooth or a shingly bottom or lies on oyster- or scallop-beds, are the favourite ground for the amateur dredger; and these will generally yield him abundance of sport for the length of a summer-day.

Those who have never seen a *dredge* may wish to have one described. There are several varieties of the instrument. The common one, with a single scraper, being in use among the fishermen on most parts of the coast, needs no description, as it may generally be had by inquiring of your boatman; but there is another kind, to which the name of *Naturalist's Dredge* may be given, which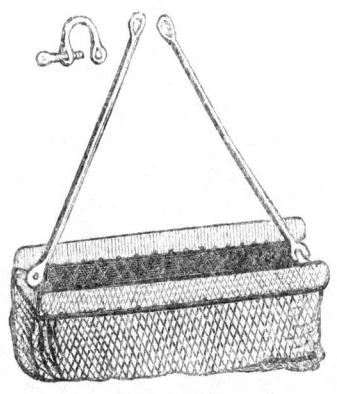

NATURALIST'S DREDGE.

possesses some advantages over the common dredge, and which can only be had by ordering it specially of a blacksmith. This kind was first recommended many years ago by Mr. Robert Ball, the well-known zoologist, and its value has been largely tested, especially in deep-sea dredging. It is an iron rectangular frame, made with a scraper at *each* side, and having a bag attached to it in the usual manner. Its handles are moveable, being connected by eyelet holes with the bars of the frame below, and united, where they join above, by a ring and screw, so that when you wish to pack up the dredge, the handles, on the ring being unscrewed, fold up, and the whole fits into a small compass. This compactness is one advantage of this kind of dredge, as it renders it much more easy of carriage. But its great value lies in the double scraper, which makes it a matter of no consequence on which side the instrument is thrown down. It cannot be reversed. The top and bottom being alike, it is a matter of indifference which shall scrape the ground. In working with a common dredge, if the instrument be not carefully thrown down it is very liable to overset, and unless it fall with the scraper in the proper position, it will not collect anything. The Naturalist's Dredge cannot overset, because either side scrapes equally well. And this, when dredging in deep water, is a quality of the greatest value.

We will suppose the dredger afloat, on a fine day and in a favourable locality, furnished with his dredge, and with some collecting boxes and bottles, and a sieve to sort the smaller animals from the mud and silt. When the water is clear and not very deep, the aspect of the bottom, as the boat glides quietly over it, often affords a charming submarine picture, as well as reveals the places where the dredge may be most profitably thrown down. The larger sea-weeds, seen like a forest waving in the clear water below you, generally mark the position of rocks, and forbid the use of the dredge; but often the treasures of such ground may be rifled by using another instrument, called a *drag*, which can sometimes be employed on foul ground with much effect.

This instrument consists of a series of hooks attached to a transverse bar and connected with a rope. It ought to weigh at least five or six pounds. This is to be dragged along among the leaves of the large sea-weeds, care being taken, when the ground is very foul, not to allow it to fall into holes among the rocks, in which it would be liable to be caught. By suffering it to drag among the sea-weeds, some of these will be detached, and being caught by the hooks, may readily be hauled up; and such leaves often afford a rich harvest. The stems and fronds of the Great Oar-weed are very generally clothed with smaller Algæ, of which many species are to be obtained only on them. The beautiful *Ptilota plumosa* is altogether confined to the stems of *Laminaria digitata*, and these stems are also the favourite habitat of many other of the more delicate *Floridæ*. *Callithamnion Pluma*, a minute but very beautiful species, forms upon them a covering resembling fine crimson velvet; *Delesseria ruscifolia; Rhodymenia palmetta*, and *Polysiphonia urceolata*, are also commonly to be met with. The number of marine animals attached to these weeds is also considerable. Several of the Sertularian and

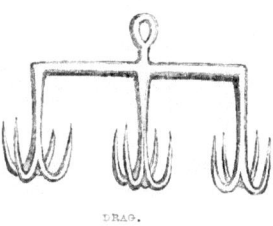
DRAG.

other Zoophytes; various and beautiful kinds of *Botryllus* and of other compound Ascidians, as well as several of the Gasteropodous Molluscs, may be collected either on the broad leaves or among the roots of the Laminariæ. Two kinds of Patella (*P. pellucida* and *P. lævis*), both remarkable for longitudinal streaks of iridescent colours on an olive shell, may be found feeding on the Laminariæ; the former generally upon the broad leaves,—the latter among the fibres of the root, or upon the fleshy stem, and very frequently within the bulb of *L. bulbosa*. To the labours of these little Molluscs may, indeed, be partly attributed the annual destruction of these gigantic Algæ. Eating into the lower part of the stems, and destroying the branches of the roots, they so far weaken the base, that it becomes unable to support the weight of the frond; and thus the plant is detached and driven on shore by the waves.

At depths beyond which the Laminariæ cease to vegetate,—that is, from about four to ten fathoms, —the bottom of the sea is frequently covered with a vegetation of a very different character, which, indeed, will scarcely be taken, by a hasty observer, to belong to the vegetable kingdom at all. In speaking of Corallines in a former chapter, I alluded to a kindred race of vegetables, called Nullipores or Melobesiæ, of a stony character, whose outward coating and much of whose interior fabric, are composed of carbonate of lime, secreted in their cells, and forming an organized portion of their bodies. Vegetables of this class bear a striking resemblance to the skeletons of some of the larger calcareous Zoophytes, especially to some of the Celleporæ;

NULLIPORES.

but they may always be known from true Zoophytes by the absence of pores, or polype-cells, in the surface; and when their structure is carefully examined with a microscope, their vegetable nature is still more obvious. To examine one of the Nullipores, it is necessary that a portion of the specimen intended for examination be first macerated for some time in dilute muriatic acid. This will dissolve the opake carbonate of lime which fills the cells, and leave the tissue in a state in which minute portions of it may readily be dissected, and placed under the microscope. It will then be found of

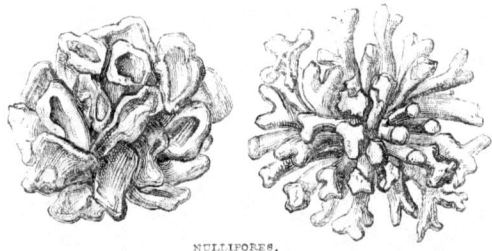

NULLIPORES.

a nature precisely similar to the cellular tissue of other Algæ. In their outer aspect the Nullipores are of very various characters. Some of them resemble Lichens in form, being thin as paper, expanding into leafy lobes, and forming circular patches on the surface of rocks. In others the leafy lobes stand erect, or are laid one beside another in globose masses, something like the gills of a mushroom. Others are much more solid, and resemble masses of smooth calcareous rock, here and there rising into wart-like prominences; and others again are very much branched, like stony trees or shrubs. When growing, the colour of the frond is more or less of a livid purple, becoming, on the death of the plant, of a brick-dust hue. Various others of the smaller Algæ, and a considerable number of marine animals, may be collected on the Nullipore-banks. Among the Algæ which especially frequent the Nullipores, one of the most interesting is *Padinella parvula*, an olive, Lichenoid species, very frequently found attached to various Nullipores. *Polysiphonia parasitica*, *P. subulifera*, and *P. furcellata*, are also among the rarities frequently found in this locality; and the more common plants are *Rhodymenia bifida*, *R. ciliata*, and broad varieties of *Dictyota dichotoma*. Among animals, several of the Annelides, and some of the Naked Molluscs, will reward the zoologist; and the collector of minute shells may secure several of the *Rissoæ* on this ground. Banks of Nullipores are, however, not very prolific; and though they afford sufficient interest for a few hauls of the dredge, and are therefore always worth a visit, their variety is soon exhausted, and the dredger soon satiated. Very frequently, also, a large portion of the bank consists of dead fronds, and these yield little to interest the explorer.

A more fertile ground for the dredger is found on the borders of scallop- or oyster-banks, the former being generally at a depth below the level at which most marine plants vegetate, though an occasional straggler here and there maintains its ground. On scallop-banks, in from ten to fifteen or twenty fathoms, the variety of marine animals is so great, that the dredge rarely comes up without bringing with it some object to interest the dredger. These are of many races, extending upwards from the simplest members of the animal kingdom, the Sponges, to the more highly organized Molluscs. In so great a variety, I can notice only a few of the more striking species.

I shall begin with an animal of a very low type of structure, the *Planaria*. Of this genus some species are found in the sea, though the majority are natives of fresh water, where they may be seen gliding over the stems and leaves of water plants, and among the threads of Confervæ, feeding on such small animals as come in their way, and as they are able to overcome. The species represented in our figure was taken on the west coast of Ireland. It was about two inches long, of an oval form, very thin and flat, of a milky

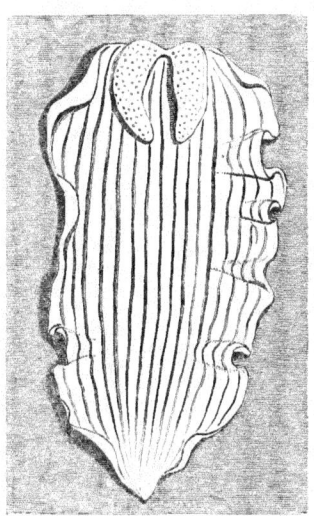

PLANARIA VITTATA.

white colour, marked with narrow longitudinal stripes or lines, of a dark-brown or blackish hue. It had two ear-like appendages at its broader end; and its other extremity, or tail, was somewhat pointed. The ears were curved backwards, and finely dotted with minute specks. It moved along with some rapidity, chiefly by contraction of the margin, which was more or less curled while the body kept in motion. On being captured, it was put into a bottle of sea-water, in company with some other animals, for the purpose of further examination; but one of these (I am uncertain which) attacked, and actually eat off about half the body of the *Planaria* before it was detected. The latter, however, seemed to feel no inconvenience from the loss of its hinder parts, and moved about as rapidly, and with as much apparent ease and pleasure, as if nothing had occurred. This insensibility to mutilation is a common character of these animals, and seems to show that they have really, as well as apparently, no nervous centres. It is well known that if a *Planaria* be cut in pieces, all the several parts will continue to live and move about; and each of them, however small, will, in due time, become a perfect animal, complete in all its parts. But what is still more curious, it has been observed that if the *Planaria* be mutilated while in motion, its separate parts will continue to move in the same direction as the animal had been following before the mutilation. This is a very curious fact, as the parts of most other animals which are similarly vivacious, when broken up, move off in opposite directions. According to the observation of anatomists, the flesh of the *Planaria* is of a very simple structure, nearly gelatinous, with little or no trace of muscular fibre; and no traces of nervous filaments have been clearly ascertained. Some species, however, have coloured specks at the anterior end of the body; and these have been supposed to be eyes, though no proof of their being organs of vision has been discovered. There is but one aperture, which serves the place both of mouth and vent. This communicates with a much-branched stomach, where the food is received and digested; and the undigested matter is rejected by being driven back by the way through which it came. Besides this digestive apparatus, there is a rudimentary vascular system, consisting of a delicate network of vessels ramifying through the body. Such is the simple arrangement of parts in these animals. They were formerly placed near the Leeches, which are of a much higher type of structure, though externally somewhat similar; but they are now arranged with the intestinal worms, to which their structure nearly allies them. None of the *Planariæ*, however, are found in the bodies of other animals.

A considerable number of the class of ANNELIDES—the group to which the Common Earth Worm and the Leech belong—are natives of the sea, and many of them are objects of great beauty. Some are curious in their structure; and others, equally curious and beautiful, are sought after by fishermen to be used as bait. All these animals have so much general resemblance to each other, that it requires little observation to recognize any as belonging to the group, when you are once familiar with any member of it. They are all of a long, generally a worm-like form, capable of contracting considerably in length, and of extending the body again. The body is composed of a set of rings or joints, connected by a common flexible skin or covering; and every joint, except the first, which serves as a head, and the last, which constitutes the tail, is precisely like the one above or below it, save in size; those of the middle portion of the body being frequently larger than the rest. The head is frequently furnished with eyes, and with more or less perfectly formed tentacula, or feelers. It contains the mouth, which in many species is armed with formidable jaws, or with cutting teeth, which furnish these voracious creatures with a powerful means of attacking their prey. Most, if not all, of them are carnivorous. The blood-sucking propensities of some, as of the Common Leech, are proverbial. The blood of all these worms is remarkable for its red colour, and it circulates through a double system of arteries and veins. The mode in which this blood is aërated varies considerably in different members of the class; and as the differences of breathing apparatus indicate important varieties of habit among these animals, these differences have been happily chosen by Cuvier, as the basis on which his systematic division of ANNELIDES, or Red-blooded Worms, is constructed. He divides this class of animals into three groups or orders. In the first, which he calls *Abranchiata*, there is no external breathing apparatus; but along the sides of the body are disposed a number of minute holes, by which the surrounding medium, be it air or aërated water, is freely admitted into little bags, concealed beneath the skin. Over the membranous surface of these bags the blood-vessels form a delicate network, by which the contained fluid is exposed, through the thin membranous wall, to the action of the air or water. To this group belong the Earth Worms, the Leeches, and several creatures of similar habits, frequenting muddy places in æstuaries and rivers. In the second family, or *Dorsibranchiata*, external breathing organs, or gills, often resembling beautiful feathery tufts, are attached in pairs either to every segment of the body, or to a certain number of the middle segments. These organs sometimes display the most elegant varieties of form and the richest colours, and afford, by their minor variations, excellent characters for classifying the smaller groups or genera. To this order belong the majority of the marine *Annelides;* and among the rest, the *Arenicola piscatorum* (Lug Worm), so commonly used as bait by fishermen. Lastly, there is the family called *Tubicola*, which differs from the two preceding groups in being composed of sedentary animals. In both the former orders the animals possess considerable activity: as the Earth Worm, which pushes its way through the soil, in which it excavates extensive galleries ; or, as the Leech, which progresses by successive steps by means of the suckers attached to its head and tail: or as the individuals of the Dorsibranchiate order, which creep along by means of the bristly oars attached to each joint of the body, or swim through the water by the help of the same organs. But in the *Tubicola* we find a set of animals which have partly the aspect of Earth Worms, partly that of Dorsibranchiate Worms, yet which differ from both in having the greater part of their body enclosed in a more or less perfectly formed tube or shell, which is permanently attached to some extraneous object. When the animal has once taken up its position, it remains fixed throughout its life. The greater part of the body being enclosed in the sheath, we do not find the gills or breathing-holes distributed throughout its length, where, indeed, they could scarcely be of any use; but we find them confined to the uppermost segments, or head, round which they form a most elaborate and richly-tinted collar of lace, which even Queen Elizabeth herself might have been proud to wear.

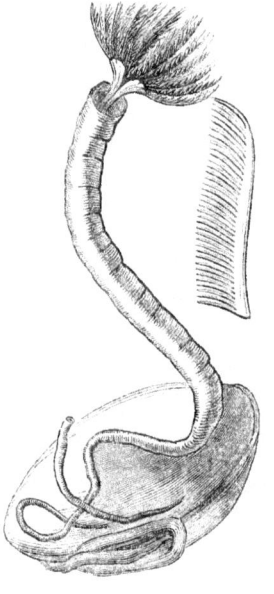

SERPULA.

Some of the commonest, as well as most perfect, examples of the order *Tubicola*, are the various kinds of *Serpula;* the smaller species of which may be found on almost every sea-weed, at least on all the more coarsely-growing kinds, as well as on every object which has lain for any length of time in the sea. Stones near low-water-mark; shells, whether dead or living; pieces of crockery-ware, or even iron instruments,— any substances, in short, which lie quietly at the bottom of the sea, and afford a point of attachment, are seized on in time by one *Serpula* or another as a foundation for his worm-like house. The tube in which these worms encase themselves is formed of regular shell, apparently secreted like the shells of the Mollusca, by the outer covering or skin of the animal. It rarely possesses any colour but white, and is usually opake and milky. In some species it is transparent and brilliant as glass; in some it is round, in others sharply angular; in some perfectly smooth, in others transversely wrinkled. Some species constantly coil up their tubes in a nearly regular, spiral manner, others twist them into every variety of shape. In some the tube is prostrate, in others erect; and in some it is prostrate during its early growth, and afterwards, when the animal has attained a mature size, rises upward, free and erect. Some kinds live in society, others are solitary. One of the largest of our British kinds, *S. tubularia*, represented in our figure, is very commonly brought up in the dredge, attached to old dead shells, &c., on scallop-banks. It generally is solitary, one *Serpula* occupying a shell to itself, over whose surface it first winds its way with gradually widening tube, until, having acquired nearly its full diameter, it rises from the shell with graceful bend, and prolongs its tube in an erect position to the length of three or four inches. The tube is about the thickness of a quill, of a dull white colour, cylindrical, and marked with a few transverse wrinkles at short intervals. Within this tube the animal can wholly retreat, closing the aperture by means of a shelly plate affixed to a fleshy horn, which rises at one side of the mouth. When the animal displays itself, as it opens while seeking for prey, its head, surrounded by the richly-coloured collar of gills, composed of numerous slender pieces, pectinated on their inner faces and spreading like a starry flower, is protruded for some distance from the tube; and here it waits, ready to seize on any small animal whose curiosity or misfortune may lead it within reach of its jaws.

Nor are the other members of the family *Tubicola* less curious and beautiful than the *Serpula*, although they do not construct so perfect tubes. Instead of clothing themselves with a shelly tube, secreted by their skin, these animals, called *Sabella*, *Terebella*, and *Amphitrite* form tubes composed of sand or of any small pieces of shell which they happen to come into contact with, and which, by means of a viscid matter exuded from their bodies, they glue together, so as to make a tolerably regular tubular coat. The empty tubes of a species of *Sabella* may often be found on sandy shores, heaped together along with dead shells and sea-weed, and the living worm may be found in its tube, buried in the sand near low-water-mark. These sand-tubes are neatly constructed of grains of nearly equal size, glued together into a wall not much thicker than paper. The form of the tube is cylindrical, or very narrowly funnel-shaped, the lower end being smaller, and gradually widening upwards. Other kinds dwell in society, like the *Sabella alveolata*, which forms extensive honeycombed masses, constructed of grains of sand, and attached to rocks near low-water-mark. Sometimes a wide surface of the rock is completely covered by these aggregated tubes. When the water retires, nothing is seen but the mouths of the tubes, in each of which a drop of water is generally retained; but, when the water again flows in, this sandy honeycomb is transformed into a scene of much beauty. From each aperture a neck protrudes, wreathed with concentric circles of gilded hairs, and ending in a head surmounted by a branching crown, which reflects rainbow colours. The whole resembles a bed densely covered with fairy flowers of strange shape and delicate structure.

Such are some of the commoner kinds of Tubicolar Annelides; those of the Dorsibranchiate order, which we commonly meet with in dredging, are still more beautiful, and some of them are among the most splendidly coloured objects that the animal kingdom presents to us. The rainbow tints of the humming-bird, and the metallic lustre of the gayest beetle, have their equals in many of the members of this family of worms. If we are free from associations of disgust at the worm-like body, we cannot help being struck with the beauty of its clothing, or the really graceful motions of these little animals, gliding like serpents among the crevices of rocks and shelly masses, or half swimming, half crawling along the bottom of a rock-pool. Naturalists, struck with their beauty and grace, have assigned to them the names of nymphs, as *Nereis, Euphrosyne, Eunice, Alciopa, Aphrodita*, and others. Our British seas furnish examples of many of these genera, but, as yet, the several species have not received, from British naturalists, that close attention which they deserve, and a monograph, illustrated by figures, is much wanted for their elucidation.

A great variety of species, varying in size and form, may be observed in dredging. One of these, which seldom fails to attract the dredger's notice by the lustre of its coat, though its frequency may cause it to be thrown back as of no value, is the Sea Mouse, or *Aphrodita* (*Halithea*) *aculeata,* which is frequently met with in dredging over muddy ground. The body of this creature is oval, three or four inches in length, or sometimes more, soft, dull grey, clothed with a fine silky substance on the back, and thinly covered with small hairs which reflect rainbow colours. The sides are broadly margined with several rows of stiff purple spines, among which are long silky hairs half an inch to an inch in length, of metallic lustre, and reflecting the most brilliant prismatic colours. Oranges and greens of the richest tints are the most abundant. Under the silky hairs of the back are concealed fifteen pairs of scaly plates, one of which is affixed to each ring of the body, and covers over the branchial organs or gills. The under surface is smooth, transversely divided into about forty rings or segments. Each segment is produced at the margin into a short fleshy lobe or oar-like body, armed with a triple row of stiff spines. These oars, or feet (for they answer partly the purposes of swimming, partly those of crawling), may be contracted at the will of the animal into conical lumps, and the spines may be wholly withdrawn, each within its proper sheath. The spines are curious microscopic weapons, each armed with barbed teeth like those of a fish-spear, capable of inflicting a severe wound on any soft body.

No one can have thrown down the dredge many times, on almost any sort of ground, and failed to bring up one or other of the various animals called Star-fishes, whose name sufficiently indicates their form. Sometimes the dredge comes up literally filled with these creatures, thousands being brought up in a single haul, as if the bottom were formed of a living bank of them, or as if we had disturbed a submarine hive in the process of swarming. The countless myriads of living Star-fishes which thus cluster together may serve to explain to us the profusion with which similar animals, whose remains are now found in rocky strata, were dispersed through the waters of the early world. But, while we have this similarity in relative quantity between the modern races and those of ancient days, we find in this, as in most other cases, a complete change in the types most common at different periods of the world's age. The animals which represent our Star-fishes in early strata have wholly perished from the modern waters; and the very type of structure to which they belonged has nearly become extinct, and is now confined to a very few species. In the seas which once flowed over the British Islands there lived a race of Star-fishes whose bodies were affixed, like flowers, to a slender stalk, composed of numerous shelly plates, disposed like the bones in a vertebral column, and connected together and rendered flexible by the fleshy coat of the animal. This stalk was fixed to some foreign body, and thus the Star-fish remained at anchor, ready to seize upon any animal which came within the length of its tether, but, unlike its modern representative, unable to pursue its game to any distance. The petrified remains of these curious animals are commonly called *Lily Stones*, or Encrinites, and the joints of their stem are known by the name of "St. Cuthbert's beads." Whether they became, at any period of their life, free from the stalk, and capable of independent motion, is uncertain, as we have no living species to tell the tale; and, to judge by the remains found in a fossil state, it does not appear probable. The modern seas of Britain furnish us with but a single species of the family *Crinoidæ*, the group to which the Lily Stars of early times belonged; and it is not a little curious that this species, though it afterwards becomes free, swimming about like any other Star-fish, is in its infancy affixed to a stalk perfectly analogous to that of the Encrinite.

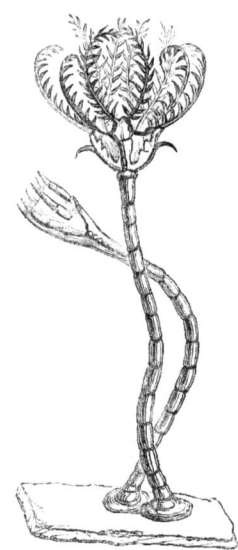

PENTACRINUS EUROPEUS.

When first detected, in this young state, it was, indeed, supposed to be a distinct animal, and believed to be the pigmy representative of the Lily Star. Subsequent observations have shown that the little creature is merely the young of the Feather Star (*Comatula rosacea*), the only living Crinoid Star-fish in the British seas.

Young Feather Stars, or, as they were called, *Pentacrinus Europeus*, are found affixed to the stems of various Zoophytes. They are about half an inch or three-quarters in height, with a body more or less resembling (according to its age) the perfect *Comatula*, fixed to a column consisting of several pentagonal joints, attached by an expanded base to the Zoophyte. The column is perfectly flexible, and can be moved at the will of the animal in any direction. Mr. J. V. Thompson, who originally discovered this curious little creature, subsequently succeeded in tracing its developement until he found the lily-shaped body had acquired most of the characters of the youngest *Comatula* which he could procure in a free state, and was thus led to the conclusion, which the observations of other naturalists have since confirmed, that the supposed *Pentacrinus* was merely the young of the *Comatula*, or Feather Star.

The Feather Star itself is certainly the most beautiful of our Star-fishes, but must be seen in a state of life and activity, as it rises in the dredge, to have all its beauties appreciated. Like so many of its kindred, it is exceedingly fragile, breaking up shortly after it finds itself in captivity, so that it can rarely, even with the greatest care, be brought to shore in an uninjured state. The body is small, clothed on the back with dense jointed filaments, and having five long slender arms cloven nearly to the base, and thus looking like ten, each branch being closely feathered with slender processes of a very elaborate structure. The whole body is of a deep rose-colour, and resembles, when its arms are expanded, a beautiful living flower, every part of which seems alive with independent motions. It would be vain to attempt in a woodcut to give a just impression of such an object, and mere description can afford but a feeble notion of its wondrous beauty. The Feather Star is found all round our coasts, and is frequently brought up in from ten to twenty fathoms water, attached to different kinds of sea-weed, which it lays hold of by means of the claws, which tip the filaments that clothe its body.

Professor Forbes's second family, the *Ophiuridæ*, are those which are now most abundant in the British seas, and whose remains, were the bottom of our ocean now converted into rock, would be found in the greatest plenty through its marbles. It is these that come up in the dredge in such vast profusion; yet the different kinds are not numerous, only twelve having been as yet noticed on the British shores. They are easily recognised from the true Star-fishes by their small round bodies, from which issue five long serpent-like or worm-like legs, which are armed with spines, and move about in all directions. When the creature swims or crawls about, either of which motions it can effect with great ease, its long legs twist and wriggle, or lash the water like whips, while the spines serve as additional locomotive organs over flat surfaces. The British species are classed under two genera, the OPHIURÆ, or Sand Stars, of which two kinds inhabit our shores, and the OPHIOCOMÆ, or Brittle Stars, of which we possess ten. These last are the most characteristic of the type, some of them having legs (if we may so call them) several inches long, and no thicker than small whipcord, with round bodies half an inch in diameter. The rays of such species remind us, as Professor Forbes well remarks, of so many Centipedes or Annelides attached, at regular distances, round a little Sea Urchin. All these animals are very brittle, and if not plunged, immediately on being gathered, into freshwater, so as to cause instant death, it is impossible to prevent their falling in pieces.

In the true Star-fishes, or *Asteriadæ*, the body itself is divided into rays like those of a star. The rays are channeled on their lower surface, and pierced by holes, through which protrude a multitude of suckers, that serve for organs of prehension, to grasp food, and for organs of motion to enable the animal to change its position. It is exceedingly curious to watch the activity that exists among these numberless sucking feet when a living Star-fish is placed on its back in a shallow vessel of water. If it have previously been touched on the lower surface, all the feet will have recoiled within the body, leaving nothing visible but a series of minute tubercles; but, when the Star-fish is allowed to recover its ease, they will quickly issue, like so many worms, from their holes, and, after moving backwards and forwards through the water, will bend round in the direction of the nearest ground: those that first reach it will affix their suckers, and by contracting will pull down a portion of the body, so as to enable others to attach themselves, until, a sufficient number of suckers being attached, their conjoint power is sufficient to bring round the body of the Star-fish to its proper position. These sucking-feet, or *cirrhi*, are tubular, and filled with fluid when fully extended. The mechanism by which they are extended is very simple. Each is connected with a globular vesicle contained within the body of the Star-fish immediately beneath the hole from which the sucker issues. When the animal wishes to extend the feet, the sides of the vesicle forcibly contract, and in so doing propel the fluid which they contain into the tubular feet, which then elongate and become tense; and when it desires to withdraw them, a contraction of its muscles drives back the fluid into the concealed vesicle. By this alternate action all the necessary motions are obtained. The skeleton of a Star-fish, or that part which remains when all the soft flesh has been removed, is a wonderfully beautiful structure, consisting of hundreds of nicely-fitted calcareous pieces arranged in a regular pattern, perfectly symmetrical in all its parts. We cannot undertake to write a description of such a skeleton, which resembles a piece of crochet-work; but one may easily be procured by any person who will take the trouble to pick up a Star-fish on the shore, and place it for some days in an ant-hill. These nimble anatomists will soon remove all the soft parts, and polish the bones with the greatest care, without injuring or displacing the minutest portion of the shell. An interesting series of specimens might be obtained by preparing such skeletons of all our native kinds.

The British species of true Star-fishes are fourteen, which are considerably more varied in character than the OPHIURIDÆ, or Brittle Stars. In the latter group we have but two generic types; but in the former there are no less than eight, distinguished from each other by characters taken from the outline of the body, the number of rows of sucking feet, and the arrangement of the spines covering the surface and bordering the avenues.* These differences are readily seen, and the groups indicated by them appear naturally associated. One of the most beautiful of the commoner kinds is the Sun Star *(Solaster papposa)*, whose disc is surrounded

* Forbes's " Starfishes," p. 75, &c.

by twelve or thirteen broad rays, and the whole of the upper surface covered with tubercles; each tubercle crowned with a tuft of eighteen or twenty long striated spines. The colours are variable, but generally brilliant. Frequently the whole is a brilliant red; sometimes the disc is red, and the rays white, and sometimes the whole surface is deep purple. Professor Forbes once took a specimen, in which the body was of a fine red, while the spiniferous tubercles were bright green. Very different in aspect from the Sun Star is the Birdsfoot Sea Star (*Palmipes membranaceus*), one of the most singular of our native species. In this the body is pentagonal, with very blunt angles, separated by wide and shallow sinuses, and the whole is so exceedingly thin that it looks more like a piece of shagreened skin than anything else. The colour is white, with a red centre and five red rays proceeding one to each angle. The whole upper surface is covered with tufts of minute spines, arranged in rows. Lastly, I may mention the Lingthorn (*Luidia fragilissima*), the largest and one of the most interesting of our British species, and very different in aspect from either of those already noticed. It appears to be peculiar to the British seas, and has been taken on various parts of the coast. Those that I have seen in a living state were dredged on the Galway coast. This Star-fish measures at least two feet across. Its body is deeply divided into five or seven lobes, which taper much to the extremity, and are many times longer than the breadth of the disk. The upper surface is perfectly flat, and densely clothed with minute tufted spines, while the margins of the lobes are fringed with several rows of longer spines. The suckers are very long and active. The colour is an orange or brick-red on the upper surface, and on the lower a pale yellow. But the most curious circumstance connected with this Star-fish, and which indicates an analogy to the Brittle Stars, is the power which it possesses of breaking itself to pieces under the influence of rage or despair. Professor Forbes gives the following amusing account of its propensities:

"Never having seen one before, and quite unconscious of its suicidal powers, I spread it out on a rowing bench, the better to admire its form and colours. On attempting to remove it for preservation, to my horror and disappointment, I found only an assemblage of rejected members: my conservative endeavours were all neutralized by its destructive exertions, and it is now badly represented in my cabinet by an armless disc and a discless arm. Next time I went to dredge on the same spot, determined not to be cheated out of a specimen in such a way a second time, I brought with me a bucket of cold fresh water, to which article Star-fishes have a great antipathy. As I expected, a *Luidia* came up in the dredge, a most gorgeous specimen. As it does not generally break up before it is raised above the surface of the sea, cautiously and anxiously I sunk my bucket to a level with the dredge's mouth, and proceeded in the most gentle manner to introduce *Luidia* to the purer element. Whether the cold air was too much for him, or the sight of the bucket too terrific, I know not; but in a moment he proceeded to dissolve his corporation, and at every mesh of the dredge his fragments were seen escaping. In despair I grasped at the largest, and brought up the extremity of an arm, with its terminating eye, the spinous eyelid of which opened and closed with something exceedingly like a wink of derision."*

The dismembered fragments of the *Luidia* continue active long after their dispersion. The feet move about and attach themselves to any object that comes within their reach, retracting and pushing out with as much vigour as they did when the creature was entire. A similar irritability is often seen in the dismembered portions of other of the lower animals which indulge in these " destructive" propensities.

The Star-fishes possess a curious organ, whose use has not hitherto been satisfactorily ascertained by anatomists. Its position is indicated externally by a sort of wart, placed on some part of the upper surface of the disc and marked with radiating striæ, resembling the plates of a Madrepore or the gills of a Mushroom. This body is commonly called the *madreporiform tubercle*. When the animal is cut open, a curved calcareous column, composed of minute hexagonal plates, united together into larger, joint-like portions, and invested with a skin, is seen connecting the inner surface of the tubercle with the plates about the mouth. After mentioning the various offices attributed to it, none of which appear satisfactory, Mr. Forbes seems inclined to regard it, with Dr. Coldstream, as the analogue of the stalk of the Crinoid Star-fishes; an opinion which will be acceptable to all who delight to contemplate the unities of nature. We leave the uses of this curious organ untold—to be determined by future observation; but we see in its

* Forbes's "Star-fishes," p. 138.

structure a memory kept up of an organ which is more fully developed in a kindred race.

The Star-fishes are closely connected with another family, which differs chiefly in the more condensed form of the body, and the more perfect solidification of its shelly coat. I mean the SEA URCHINS, of which more kinds than one frequently come up in the dredge. The common Egg Urchin (*Echinus sphæra*), the largest and best known of our British species, may be taken as an example of the race. On comparing one of these Urchins with a Star-fish, such as the *Luidia*, there is, at first sight, so little outward similarity, that we should scarcely suppose their close connexion. But the more we examine them, the greater is the number of points which we establish between them:—the rows of sucking feet common to both; the radiating lines in which all the organs are disposed, and the correspondence between the compartments into which the body is divided. There remains, in the opposite scale, the difference of form. But when we examine a series of Star-fishes, we find a beautiful gradation of form, in which those with the longest rays are insensibly connected with others which are scarcely more radiated than some Urchins. There are flat, discoid Urchins, and others of every degree of convexity, till we come to the globose form of our Sea Egg. We have also, in the Sea Eggs, the representative of the madreporiform tubercle of the Star-fishes, in a state certainly much reduced, but sufficiently obvious. So that, on the whole, the evidence in favour of the close affinity of these two families of animals greatly outweighs that against their connexion.

The Egg Urchin (*Echinus sphæra*) is so well known that I scarcely need enter into a minute description of its form. As commonly seen ornamenting the chimney-pieces of cottages near the sea-side, it is a slightly depressed sphere, divided, by five double rows of minute holes (called *ambulacra*), into ten gore-shaped spaces, of which each alternate one is twice as broad as the other. These spaces are moreover studded with rows of pearls, arranged with much regularity, and of various sizes. When the animal was alive, a short white spine, used by the Urchin as an organ of motion, or of defence, was articulated by a socket-joint to each pearly tubercle, which formed the ball on which it freely revolved. From each pair of holes of the *ambulacra* issued a sucker, like that of the Star-fish, and used for the same purposes. So that the Urchin, which now looks so armless and bald, was furnished with hundreds, nay, thousands, of active organs, arms or legs, as he required them. Nor were these by any means *all* the apparatus with which he was provided. On the surface of his coat, among the spines, were multitudes of exceedingly minute and beautifully-formed *pincers*, which were in perpetual action, moving about from side to side, and opening and shutting their three-forked apex continually. These most singular organs, which are also found on some Star-fishes, are called by naturalists *pedicellariæ;* but their use to the animal is wholly unknown, and by some writers they are described as parasitic creatures of different species. I can hardly so regard them, and, whatever their office may be, must suppose them a part of the animal on which they are found. The annexed drawing will give a general idea of their appearance in the Egg Urchin. They are of three kinds, differing from each other in the form of the *head*. Below, a hard, calcareous column, slightly knobbed at each end, enclosed by the stalk, which is slender there; but, where the column ends, widens into what is called the *neck*. This part, composed of a tough skin, is quite transparent, and very flexible, and while life continues it bends about in all

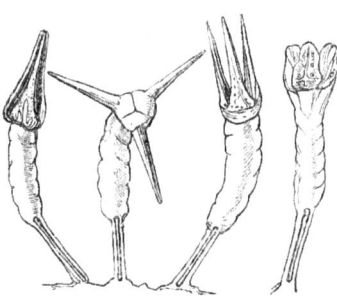

PEDICELLARIÆ.

directions. At the summit of this *neck* is a convex head, crowned with three hard, calcareous teeth, beautifully sculptured, and of three principal shapes; some long and slender, others short and very obtuse. A more full account of their history and structure will be found in Forbes's "Star-fishes," p. 155—159.

The shell of the Egg Urchin is not at all less curious than the organs with which it is clothed. The globose box in which the softer parts of the animal are shut up, is by no means the simple crustaceous body which, at first sight, it may seem to be; but is built up of several hundreds of pieces, accurately fitted together, like the fragments which compose a fine piece of mosaic work. The lines which separate them are scarcely visible, without close inspection; but the shell may easily be, if allowed to macerate for some days in fresh water, broken up into its component parts. These will be found to be of various sizes and shapes, in different parts of the shell, but nearly all are pentagonal, and one so nicely fitted to the other, that no minute space is left without its covering. The very complex structure of this shell may at first seem to be a waste of skill, an expenditure of contrivance uncalled-for by the wants of the creature. But we may be assured that there is no such waste in Nature; and, in the present instance, the structure is easily accounted for, and may be shown to be the best which could be devised to answer the required purpose. It is required to form a globose shell sufficiently hard to afford protection to the soft parts of the animal, and so constructed that it will gradually enlarge, with the growth of the creature, without any alteration of form. A simple crust would not answer these purposes, for, once formed and hardened, it would be incapable of further growth. A crust, composed of a multitude of pieces, as this is, completely answers the purpose; for the whole body may be caused to increase in growth, with the greatest regularity, by constant minute additions to the edges of the several pieces. And this is the method by which the shell of the Urchin does increase. If we examine a living Urchin, we shall find that every portion of the surface of the shell, and even of the spines, is coated over with a delicate living membrane, and that this membrane insinuates itself between each of the pieces of the shell, however closely pressed together they appear. In this membrane resides the faculty of secreting the carbonate of lime for the formation of shell, and this, as fast as it is secreted, is deposited, layer after layer, round the edges of each plate, so that these are constantly enlarging during the active growth of the animal, till it has attained its full size. The spines are deposited in the same way, by the membrane which clothes them, and exhibit, in their structure, as seen in the microscope, the most exquisitely beautiful and regular arrangement of particles that can well be conceived. Under the ceaseless activity of the vital power, the deposition of shelly matter proceeds, and results in a structure whose exactness and beauty it would be vain to imitate.

The bony contents of the shell are not at all less elaborate; and when we consider the apparently low grade of the animal for whose use they are designed, and the simplicity of other parts of its organization, we cannot fail to be struck with wonder at the amount of skill and contrivance lavished on its dental apparatus. The prehension of food is certainly the first requirement of animal life, and consequently we find the organs connected with its mastication and digestion,—the mouth and stomach,—those that are most prominently developed in the lower animals. Some of these appear to be mere stomachs, endowed with a capacious gullet, and a set of sucking lips. In others, the organs for cutting or tearing food, or for grinding it to jelly, are extremely powerful; and when their strength is compared with the weakness or inertia of their other organs, they give us that impression of disproportion which leads to the idea of monstrosity, and which may, in some degree account for the disgust or horror with which we view many of these creatures. Indeed, except in their minute size, they resemble in their characters many of the fabled monsters of antiquity, whose voracity was one of their most appalling qualities. Magnify any of the insect race, or of the worms to the size of elephants or serpents, and what portentous monsters they become! Their mouths and jaws seem utterly disproportionate in strength and complexity to the rest of their structure, though not at all disproportionate to the office which these scavengers of creation discharge in the general scheme. But few animals can boast a dental apparatus equal in complexity to that of the Egg Urchin; a set of harder-pointed teeth; more grinding jaws, with a surface regularly "dressed," like that of a millstone; or stronger and more varied muscular bands, by which the motions of the whole structure are regulated. In an Urchin of the usual size this system of bony jaws and teeth forms a conical body, about an inch and a half long, placed with its pointed end toward the large aperture at the base of the shell, and extending backwards into the body of the animal. It is attached by strong muscles to five bony arches that surround the mouth of the shell, and several other sets of muscles serve to propel it forward, to cause it to retreat, to move the mass from side to side, or to cause the jaws to act one on another, like pairs of millstones. The cone consists of five triangular pieces or jaws, hollowed out, with an opening down the centre in front; arched behind, and with the two sides flattened and finely grooved. In the hollow of these jaws is placed a long moveable tooth, which plays up and down. When the cone is put together, the flat, dressed surfaces of the five jaws, which stand round in a circle, are brought into contact. All the food which is received at the mouth must pass between these surfaces; and as there are systems of muscles which enable them to play up and down and across, a more perfect mill for grinding down the food cannot well be conceived. We have not space more fully to describe it, but the excellent popular account given by Professor Jones,* and the examination of a living specimen, will enable any one to understand the uses of the several parts of this singular mechanism.

Of the same class with the Sea Urchins and Starfishes, but exhibiting its characters in a weaker degree, and showing in form and structure a tendency towards the Annelides, are the *Holothuriadæ*, or Sea Cucumbers, of which several species occasionally come up in the dredge. Their name, Sea Cucumbers, is very expressive of their form in a contracted state, when the body shrinks up into an oblong mass, slightly tapering to each end, and rough with wrinkles and with the rows of sucking-feet, which it has in common with the Urchins and Star-fishes. In its texture it is tough and leathery, without calcareous plates. The absence of a shell, the presence of feathery tentacula about the mouth, and the shape of the body, are differences between these creatures and the Urchins; while the two latter circumstances, together with the mode of progression by alternate contractions and extensions of the body, connect them with the Annelides. The general form of this

* "General Outline of the Animal Kingdom," p. 166, &c.

THYONE PAPILLOSA. 149

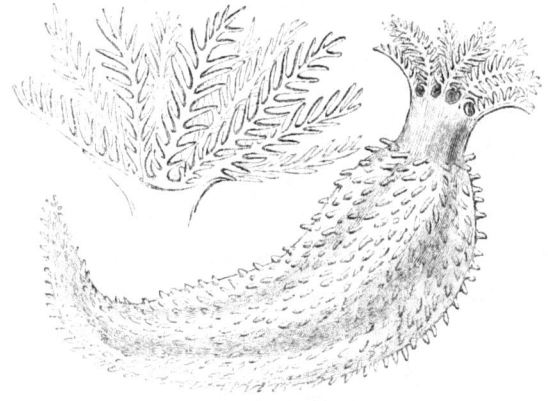

THYONE PAPILLOSA.

family may be understood from the annexed figure, which represents *Thyone papillosa*, a species found on various parts of the coast. It differs from other animals of the family chiefly by having its sucking-feet scattered in an irregular manner over the whole surface, instead of being confined to five rows along the angles of the body. In other respects it resembles most of its kindred. Its length is about three inches, but it can at pleasure extend and contract considerably. The colour is a dusky brownish-white, sometimes varied with spots. The tentacula, commonly whitish, are ten in number, pinnate, and capable of being much expanded, or wholly retracted within the orifice of the mouth. In captivity it is not always easy to persuade it to put forth these delicate organs to their full extent, but a bath of clean water will often put it into good-humour. We have already noticed the self-destruction of some of the Star-fishes: the Sea Cucumbers have an equally singular habit of a similar kind. As their skin is too tough and strong to admit of voluntary dismemberment, they resort to the unique mode of vomiting up their intestines—in fact, the whole of their internal organs. Yet it does not appear that life is destroyed by this process. At least, it does not suddenly cease; and, according to the observations of Sir J. G. Dalyell, the lost parts are renewed, after months have elapsed, even in cases where the disembowelling process has been carried to an extreme point, leaving "the body an empty sac." Holothuriæ are often taken with their internal parts more or less deficient, yet apparently existing in health and vigour: in such, probably, the lost parts are in process of restoration.

Many interesting members of the class of Zoophytes, or compound Polypes, are met with in dredging, a general account of whose classification has been given in a former chapter. For a more specific account of the deep-sea species, I must refer to Dr. Johnston's admirable work on the subject, and will here just notice some of the other ASTEROIDA, which I purposely omitted when speaking of the other two orders, HYDROIDA and HELIANTHOIDA. This group is distinguished from either of the others by a readily seen character, namely, the softer parts of the compound animal invest and enclose the harder parts, or skeleton. The *coral* of all this group is therefore internal. The precious coral of commerce is the skeleton of one of these Zoophytes; and so is the *Gorgonia flabellum,* or Venus's Fan, a well-known West Indian species, which forms a beautiful network, strengthened by a branching system of ribs, like the ribs and fibres of a skeleton leaf. Four British species of *Gorgonia*, one of them common on the Devonshire coast, are recorded. *G. verrucosa*, the commonest of these, is from six to twelve inches high, and much branched, like a tree; but its branches do not form a network. Its coral has a dense, black axis, of a horny substance, which encloses a white pith, and is coated with a whitish crust, covered with warts, arranged in somewhat spiral lines. Such is the aspect of the dried Polypidom. When living the crust is soft and flesh-coloured. The *Alcyonium*, another member of this order, has already been noticed. More interesting and beautiful forms are found in the family of *Pennatulidæ* or Sea-pens, of which three species, arranged under as many genera, are natives of Britain. These curious animals present us with the fact of compound bodies, in all respects analogous to corals, existing in an unattached state (that is not rooted or fixed to any base, but freely planted in soft mud), and possibly capable of a motion through the water from place to place. The fact of this motion has been asserted by several naturalists, but observations are wanting in corroboration. The Sea-pen itself (*Pennatula phosphorea*) is one of the most singular and beautiful of the British Zoophytes. The Polypidom is three or four inches in length, fleshy, of a purplish-red colour, narrow and naked at the lower end, and feathered on its upper half with long, closely-set pinnæ, along the margins of which the polype-cells are placed. These pinnæ are obliquely curved backwards, and capable of separate or united motion; and they have been supposed,

VIRGULARIA MIRABILIS.

by authors who believe in the swimming powers of this Zoophyte, to have the regular oar-like motion of fins. Through the centre of the stalk runs a calcareous column, which serves to stiffen the body of the Polypidom. When irritated, this Zoophyte is brilliantly phosphorescent; but it does not emit light unless disturbed, or under the influence of pain. Professor Forbes has remarked that, when it is touched, the luminosity commences at the point of contact, and proceeds upwards to the Polypiferous portion of the Zoophyte, but never in a contrary direction; and when the centre of the polypiferous portion is struck, the Polypes below the injury are not affected, while those above it emit light. "When thrown into fresh water, the *Pennatula* scatters sparks about in all directions,— a most beautiful sight." The *Virgularia mirabilis* is another of this family, closely allied to *Pennatula*, but of a much more slender form, resembling a rod, whence its name. It is several inches long and quite straight, traversed by a cylindrical calcareous stem or column, coated with a transparent flesh. Through nearly its whole length this rod-like body is furnished with short fin-like lobes of a crescent shape, which approach in pairs, but are not strictly opposite;—they are about the eighth of an inch asunder, and are furnished along the margin with a row of urn-shaped polype-cells. These lobes have the power of contracting, so as to lie closely imbricated one on another; and of expanding to an angle of about 30°, so as to leave open spaces between. They are of a pale orange-fawn colour, gracefully curved backwards, and each contains about eight polype-cells. The Polypes are objects of great beauty, and their form may be very well seen even after death; for, though capable of retractation within the cell, the tentacula have no contractile power, and may be made to expand in their full extension by merely pressing upon the cell. The Polype thus displayed is an eight-rayed star, the rays curved backwards, channeled, and elegantly pectinated along each margin. In the centre is the mouth with prominent lips. The *Virgularia* is found chiefly in Scotland and the north of Ireland, and I have taken it recently on the Galway coast in Birturbui Bay. The only remaining British Zoophyte of this group, *Pavonaria quadrangularis*, is exceedingly rare, and has yet been taken only near Oban, on the West of Scotland. In its form it bears a considerable resemblance to the *Virgularia*, but is curved, and of much greater dimensions, the length being sometimes forty-eight inches. When irritated it emits a bluish light.

The great class of CRUSTACEA, of which Crabs and Lobsters are familiar examples, demands some notice, but is so varied in its aspect and in the numerous types which its orders, families, and genera present to us, that I cannot attempt to give, in the few pages to be devoted to the subject, even an outline sketch of its classification. I can scarcely do more than notice in this place a few of the commoner Crabs which one meets with in dredging.

The class Crustacea of modern authors was included by Linnæus among his Insects, and formed a part of the *Aptera* or wingless insects of that author. The structure of a Crab or Lobster, or a Wood-louse, which are all members of the class, does indeed in many ways resemble that of the true Insects. The body is cased with hard materials, it is divided by articulations into several rings, it is furnished with jointed legs and with those curious organs called *antennæ* or feelers, and it possesses a mouth constructed on a very similar type. There is one peculiarity, however, in which there is a remarkable difference between the Crustacea and both the Insect and Spider Classes. These latter groups of animals are destined to live in the air, and their respiration is consequently performed by lungs. Even such species of them as are aquatic carry with them under water the quantity of air necessary to their existence, just as a diver inflates his lungs before he leaves the surface; though it is quite true that some breathe through the medium of gills while they continue in a rudimentary state. The

Crustacea, being either water animals, or constantly frequenting very damp places, respire through the medium of gills. This is one important feature in their economy by which they differ from insects. Another is, that they continue to increase in bulk after they have attained the mature form of their kind. In the insect, increase in bulk, and the changes of skin which it requires, are confined to the metamorphic stages through which the animal passes, and cease when the limbs acquire their permanent form. In the Crustacean, though the earlier stages undergo metamorphoses, some of them quite as singular as those that we find among insects, the animal continues to increase in size long after its limbs have been completely formed; and the provision by which this is effected is not the least curious point in their history. Differences of this important nature, and others of a similar kind, added to the immense extent of both classes, have induced modern naturalists to separate the class Crustacea from the other articulate animals with which Linnæus combined them.

The different aspects which the gills assume in the various groups of Crustacean animals, while they afford, as in other classes, excellent classifying characters, exhibit to us some beautiful adaptations, which are quite as interesting to the unlettered observer as to the systematic naturalist. In some of the more minute individuals of the race, as in the *Water-fleas*, which may be found by myriads in any stagnant pool, the respiratory organs are seated in the legs themselves, whose covering is so delicate that it admits the vessels that ramify over it to have sufficient contact with the water to allow of the perfect aëration of the blood. This little creature may be said to breathe through its legs and arms, which may be seen in constant motion, playing through the fluid, and causing a constant flow of new particles to the exposed surface of the blood-vessels. Can we conceive a more ecstatic little being than this, whose every motion is an inspiration! at least, whose muscular efforts bear a direct proportion to the aëration of its blood; the power that is expended in every effort being renewed by the very act of making that effort. In these lowest members of the class we find the legs themselves performing the office of gills; but though among the higher types of structure, the legs are used for the more common purposes of swimming or walking, we still find the gills connected with the upper portion of the legs, where they are inserted into the body. Thus the active motions of walking and swimming contribute to the aëration of the blood, by causing a correspondent motion in the branchiæ. These organs are lodged in two chambers, situated one at each side of the under surface of the *carapace* or broad shelly plate, which freely communicate by wide openings with the water. In opening a Crab or Lobster, at table, these gills generally come off attached to the bases of the smaller legs.

The dexterity of the Crustacea in casting their shells is certainly wonderful. When one considers the hardness of the shelly coat, and the extraordinary forms which it assumes, especially the large claws terminating slender arms, and is told that all this coat of mail is annually thrown off in a single piece by the contained animal, the greatest proficient in Chinese mechanical puzzles may well be posed at this greater puzzle. One is tempted to ask, too, remembering the beautiful arrangement provided for the growth of the shell in the Sea Urchin, why something similar was not devised to assist the Crab ; why one creature should enjoy the protection of its house of defence at so little trouble, the walls gradually widening as his wants increase ; while another has, every returning season, either to burst, or by violent muscular efforts, to flay itself alive, and then wait, defenceless and naked, till a new coat grows on its back. I suppose happiness is equally distributed, and that what would be death to one animal may be sport to another! Possibly the extraordinary efforts made by the Crab or Lobster in throwing off their shells, may be attended with pleasurable sensations.

The process of moulting has been observed by the celebrated naturalist Reaumur in the fresh-water Cray-fish (*Astacus fluviatilis*), and most probably that of other kinds is effected in a similar manner. In the autumn the Cray-fish retires into a hole, where it remains for some time without food. While thus stationary, the old shell becomes gradually loosened, and a new and soft cuticle is formed beneath it. The Cray-fish is now greatly excited, and by violent efforts seeks to free its new skin from the old shell, which it is about to cast away. When this has been done, the difficulty remains of escaping from its trammels. Its limbs are so perfectly encased in armour that, at first sight, it seems impossible to escape from the confinement without breaking the shell to pieces. But the Cray-fish has no such intention. He knows that by persevering exertions he can rid himself of his burden ; and with many violent efforts, and many a weary struggle, he succeeds in getting rid, first of the carapace, or body-shell ; then of the leg-coverings ; then of the tail-piece : and, finally, of all the shelly coat, down to the coverings of the antennæ ; and even the coating of the stomach, with its curious dental apparatus. And the whole is thrown off without loosening the joints or rupturing the shell. It would be impossible for any mounter of specimens to extract the flesh with such nicety, and without injury to any portion of the case.

The power of voluntary dismemberment possessed by the Star-fishes is shared also by the Crustacea, who will cast away their legs, and even the ponderous claw-bearing arms, on being alarmed, or on suffering injury in these members ; and this without the appearance of experiencing pain, or more than temporary inconvenience. They walk away, with their remaining limbs, as if nothing particular had happened. After a time the lost portion is gradually restored, the new limb sprouting out from the stump of the old. Thus Lobsters and Crabs are frequently met with, one of whose arms is of much greater size than the other, the smaller one being evidently a second growth.

The general form of the body and the organs of locomotion are considerably varied in the different families of Crustacea, according to the habits of the animal. In some of the lower races, the body presents a series of rings, or pieces nearly of equal form and size, arranged one after another, and each furnished with a pair of crawling or swimming legs, the whole animal bearing a great resemblance to one of the Annelides, but showing a slight advance in organization. As we rise to higher and more developed forms, we find a gradual concentration of the parts of the body, effected by the more or less perfect coalition of its ring-like parts into solid pieces. At the same time, one definite idea or plan seems to pervade the whole class. According to this idea the body of a Crustacean consists of twenty-one ring-like pieces, seven of which belong to the region of the head, seven to the region of the thorax, or central part of the body, and seven to the abdominal region, commonly called the tail. In almost every case the pieces belonging to the region of the head are considerably condensed, their pairs of legs being converted into the organs of the mouth, which in this class, as in insects, is highly compound in structure. In many of the lower Crustacea, as in the Isopoda—the group to which the Wood-louse belongs, and which includes a large number of marine animals which resemble Wood-lice in form,—the joints of the thorax are distinct from each other, resembling rings, and not materially differing from those of the tail. But in the higher Crustacea, as in the Lobster, and still more in the Crab, the thoracic portion is covered externally by a single solid shelly piece. It appears like a single joint of the body, and its compound nature is only indicated by the number of pairs of legs which rise from its lower surface. In some species there is an indication of rings on the surface of the shell, more or less evident; but in others all such tokens of composition are obliterated. The joints of the abdomen or tail, which are so evident in the Lobster, are more concentrated in the Crabs; and in the singular animals called King Crabs (*Limuli*), common on the shores of warm countries, a complete concentration of the abdominal pieces takes place, a broad shield, as solid as the carapace of the Crab, being substituted for the ring-like plates. These variations of form, from the most perfect separation of parts to the most complete union, offer an interesting study; but the change must be traced through an extensive series of genera and species.

The organs of locomotion are very different in the different groups. Some Crustacea are adapted for swimming, others for crawling, and others, again, lead a nearly sedentary life, as parasites on other animals, often on fishes, and, in many cases, on the larger Crustacea themselves. The Crabs afford us an instance of the greatest compactness in the body,—the segments of the head being minute, and often concealed under the thorax, and those of the abdomen also of small size, and coiled up under the ample shield of the same portion; so that the whole body seen from above resembles a box. In this tribe five pair of legs, belonging to the thoracic portion, are largely developed, the first pair being converted into claws; and the creature can move with great ease and considerable speed on land, or crawl along the bottom of the sea. But its motion, owing to the position of the legs, is either sideways or backwards: it cannot move in a forward direction. In many Crabs, especially in those that frequent deep water, the last pair of legs have their terminal joints very much widened and flattened—in fact, converted into oars, by the help of which these Crabs swim with great ease, while the formation of their other legs permit of their crawling with equal facility when they desire it. In the Lobster, and all the long-tailed Crustacea, such as the various kinds of Shrimp and Prawn, the tail is the chief instrument of locomotion. Owing to the form of the body, these animals, notwithstanding their well-developed legs, make but slow work of it when they attempt to crawl. But nothing can exceed their activity in swimming—or, more properly, in darting backwards, —through the water. The rapid motions of a Shrimp or Prawn must be familiar to every sea-side visitant. Those of a Lobster, though less frequently seen, are equally rapid, and both are effected in the same manner. The tail in these animals is furnished at its extremity with a number of broad, flat plates, so placed as to close together when this organ is extended, and to open and present a broad fan to the water on every downward stroke. The Lobster turns his back, which is smooth and rounded, so as to present little resistance to the water, in the direction in which he wishes to move, and then by a vigorous stroke of the tail, whose front, presented to the water, is concave, and its extremity furnished with a spreading fan, he can dart backwards to the distance of eighteen or twenty feet.

Among the Crabs which one commonly meets with in dredging are several kinds, belonging to more than one modern genus, to which the popular name of Spider-Crab is given. These are all characterized by having long and slender legs like those of Spiders, and generally a triangular body, more or less pointed, or produced into a snout in front. The commonest species of these (*Stenorhyncus phalangium*) is met with on most parts of the coast, frequenting scallop-banks, and similar ground. Its body is an inch or more in length, triangular, and rough with several spines, and rising into prominences. Its legs are three or four times as long as its body, with long, slender joints, and it has a pair of stout arms, terminating in large claws. Both legs and arms are rough with hairs. Its habits are sluggish, its motions slow and feeble, and when caught it does not show fight nor make the efforts to escape, which most other Crabs do on being captured. Very frequently its shell is completely covered with a growth of sea-weeds or Zoophytes. Others of the group of Spider-Crabs have similar habits and general aspect, except that some are smooth, with fewer prominences on the shell. Leaving them, we next find the family of *Maiadæ*. These bear a considerable resemblance to the true Spider-Crab, especially in the triangular form of the body, and its usually rough surface; but their legs are stouter and less elongate. The resemblance to the Spider is still sufficiently great, and they obtain this name from fishermen. The largest of the group, *Maia squinado*, is eaten on some parts of the coast. It has an oval body, very convex, produced in front into two stout horns, and roughened over all parts of its surface with spines and tubercles of various sizes. The legs are stout, and exceedingly rough and hairy, with tuberculated joints. The claws are small, and the arms not much stouter than the legs. The family of Swimming-Crabs, or *Portunidæ*, many kinds of which are met with in dredging, offers a form of body and limbs strikingly dissimilar to those of the Spider-Crabs, and a corresponding difference of habits. In these the body is generally very broad in proportion to its length, and wider in front than it is behind. The front margin of the shell has a rounded outline, but is more or less toothed; the rostrum is broad, and but little prominent, and the eyes are widely separated. But the most striking character of the family is found in the hinder pair of legs, which are converted into oars, and used by the animal in swimming. The habits of these Crabs are much more active than those of the Spiders, their limbs much stronger, and they are all armed with a peculiarly effective pair of stout pincers. The Velvet-Crab (*Portunus puber*) is a well-known species of this family, several of which are among the most beautiful of the British Crabs. The Velvet-Crab is so named from its coat,—the whole surface of the shell, and of the legs, except some polished longitudinal ridges, being covered with a short pile of soft hairs. The colours of the living animal are a beautiful compound of reddish-brown and blue; but they soon fade after death. Some remarkable forms of body are found in the genus *Ebalia*, Crabs of small size, of which there are three British species. The carapace in these is rhomboidal, the lateral angles being much produced. It is marked with elevations and depressions, so arranged as to represent a more or less perfectly-formed face. But the most natural resemblance to a human face is found in the markings of the shell of *Corystes cassivelaunus*, called from this peculiarity the Masked-Crab by Professor Bell. It is the *Cancer personatus* of

Linnæus. In this species the length of the shell is considerably greater than its breadth, and of an oval form, with a central ridge which represents the nose, lateral depressions for the eyes, and a transverse line, bordered by broad but shallow ridges, for the mouth and lips. In some specimens the parts of this face are much more prominent than in others. The species is otherwise remarkable for the great length of its claws and of its antennæ. It generally frequents deep water, but is occasionally cast on shore.

I must not omit to notice two species of minute Crabs whose curious semi-parasitical habits have long rendered them famous. The readers of Darwin's fantastic poem must be familiar with the history of

"Pinna and her Cancer friend."

It was known to the ancients that a minute Crab sought refuge in the shell of the Pinna, and modern research has detected others which take up their residence within the shells of several other kinds of bivalves, especially of Mussels and Cockles. These little Crabs belong to the genus *Pinnotheres*, and two species are found on our coast. One of them, *P. pisum*, is very commonly found within the shell of the Common Mussel, especially when raised from deep water. Its shell is from a quarter to nearly half an inch in breadth, rounded and convex, of a thin substance and brownish colour, with one or two yellow spots. The other species, *P. veterum*, is usually found within the shell of the Pinna, and differs in being of a more angular form and uniform brown colour. The habits of both species appear to be similar.

They retreat to the shells of the Mollusca, not to feed on the animal, as a true parasite does, but, as is supposed, for protection, as other animals would take refuge in a nest or cave. The shells of these Crabs, at least of the female, are very soft and thin, and possibly this is the cause of their singular habits. It is a pity, at least for the poet, that truth obliges us to omit the romantic stories once believed regarding the mutual affection of the pair thus oddly consorted.

A highly curious fact in the history of the Crustacea relates to their metamorphoses, the young animal passing through stages as wonderful as those observed in the class of Insects. To Mr. J. Vaughan Thompson naturalists are indebted for the discovery of the metamorphic stages in the Common Crab, and several others of the order to which it belongs. Other observers have since witnessed the developement of many other species, and thus rendered it probable that all the higher Crustacea pass through similar stages of existence. Before Mr. Thompson's observations the little creatures, which are now known to be young Crabs, were considered as belonging to a distinct genus, called *Zoea*, placed in a different order of Crustacea, widely apart from the Crab-

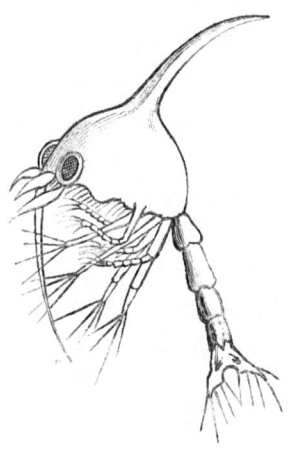

ZOEA OF THE CRAB.

family; just as a Tadpole might be placed by a person who merely regarded its form, and was ignorant of its history, in a widely different family from the parent Frog. When first hatched, the young of the Crab presents the singularly grotesque form represented in our figure. It has a helmet-shaped head, terminating behind in a long horn, and furnished in front with a pair of huge sessile eyes, and it moves through the water by means of its long swimming tail. After the first change of skin the body assumes something like its permanent shape; the eyes become stalked; the claws are developed, and the legs resemble those of the Crab; but the change is still incomplete, for the tail is still long and furnished with false feet, like that of a Lobster. The swimming habit has not yet been laid aside. At the next stage, while the little creature is still about the eighth of an inch in diameter, the crab-form is completed, the abdomen folding in under the carapace. All the subsequent changes are merely changes of coat, consequent on the growth of the now complete animal. In these several metamorphoses we see portrayed, in succession, the peculiarities of three different types, one rising above the other in structure. In the first stage the Crab resembles one of the least perfect Crustacea, such as the Water-flea; in the second it assumes the aspect of the Lobster; and finally puts on the form of the most perfect animals of the class. Thus it is that Nature advances step by step, gradually bringing out, through successive stages of being new organs and new faculties, and leaving as she moves along, at every step, some animals that rise no higher, as if to serve for land-marks of her doings through all succeeding time. And this it is that makes the study of Comparative Anatomy so fascinating. Not that I mean to favour a theory of *developement* which would obliterate all idea of species, by supposing that the more compound animal forms were developements of their simpler ancestors. For such an hypothesis Natural History affords no evidence ; but she gives us, through all her domains, the most beautiful and diversified proofs of an adherence to a settled order, in which new combinations are continually brought out. In this order, the lowest grades of being have certain characters, above which they do not rise, but propagate beings as simple as themselves. Above them are others which, passing through stages in their infancy equal to the adult condition of those below, acquire, when at maturity, a perfection of organs peculiarly their own. Others again rise above these, and thus structures become gradually more compound ; till at last it may be said that the simpler animals represent, as in a glass, the scattered organs of the higher races.

ICEBERG AND BARRIER.

CHAPTER VI.

THE MICROSCOPIC WONDERS OF THE SEA.

An eloquent modern writer, in arguing for the existence on this earth of an invisible world of spirits, draws a striking illustration of his subject from our connexion with the lower animals, whose forms we indeed see around us, but the secrets of whose being, whose motives of action, and whose final destiny, remain unfathomable mysteries. "We are," says he, " in a world of spirits, as well as in a world of sense, and we hold communion with it, and take part in it, though we are not conscious of doing so. If this seems strange to any one, let him reflect that we are undeniably taking part in a third world, which we do indeed see, but about which

we do not know more than about the angelic hosts,—
the world of brute animals. Can anything be more
marvellous or startling, unless we were used to it, than
that we should have a race of beings about us whom we
do but see, and as little know of their state, or can
describe their interests or their destiny, as we can tell of
the inhabitants of the sun and moon? It is, indeed, a
very overpowering thought, when we get to fix our
minds on it, that we familiarly use, I may say hold in-
tercourse with, creatures who are as much strangers to
us, as mysterious as if they were the fabulous, unearthly
beings, more powerful than man, yet his slaves, which
Eastern superstitions have invented. We have more
real knowledge about the angels than about the brutes.
They have, apparently, passions, habits, and a certain
accountableness, but all is mystery about them. We do
not know whether they can sin or not, whether they
are under punishment, whether they are to live after
this life. We inflict very great sufferings on a portion
of them, and they in turn, every now and then, seem to
retaliate upon us, as if by a wonderful law. We depend
on them in various important ways; we use their labour,
we eat their flesh. This, however, relates to such of
them as come near us. Cast your thoughts abroad on
the whole number of them, large and small, in vast
forests, or in the water, or in the air, and then say whether the presence of such countless multitudes, so various
in their natures, so strange and wild in their shapes,
living on the earth without ascertainable object, is not
as mysterious as anything which Scripture says about
the angels? Is it not plain to us that there is a world

inferior to us in the scale of beings, with which we are connected without understanding what it is? and is it difficult to faith to admit the word of Scripture concerning our connexion with a world superior to us?"

When we consider the animal kingdom from this point of view, and further reflect that each of the species of which it consists is as isolated from every other species, and forms to itself as much a world within its own borders, as does the human family,—the co-existence of innumerable phases of being, in the presence of each other, is more and more wonderful, and may well lead us to infer the reality of things beyond our senses to perceive, and but dimly revealed to our reason; and yet we see but a little way into the wonders of creation, if we confine our researches to objects visible to the unassisted eye.

The improvements effected of late years in the microscope, may well be said to have opened to us a material world of whose existence we should otherwise be wholly ignorant. The number of species of animals and plants now known, whose forms are so minute that they are individually invisible to the naked eye, and only appreciable when collected together in masses, is very great; and the catalogue is daily enlarging as the waters of the sea, and of lakes and ponds, are more carefully subjected to examination. What to the naked eye seems like a green or brownish slimy scum, attached to the stalks of water-plants, or floating on the surface of stagnant pools, displays to the microscope a series of elegant and curious forms, endowed with a most perfect symmetry and delicate structure of parts, each acting in the circle of its narrow sphere as perfectly as the more bulky creations above it. The great work of Ehrenberg has made the forms of many of these curious creatures sufficiently known; and a most elaborate monograph of a portion of them,* recently published in this country, has added much to the general history of the subject, while it affords to British students exquisitely accurate figures and careful descriptions of all the British species of the group illustrated.

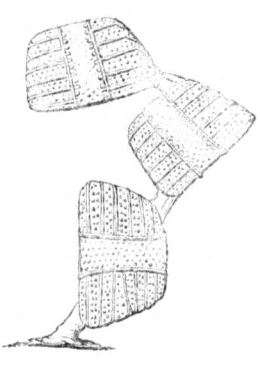

ISTHMIA OBLIQUATA.

The plants included in this microscopic world are classed by botanists under two families, the *Desmidieæ*, which exclusively inhabit fresh water, and the *Diatomaceæ*, a great number of which are marine. The forms of these minute organisms are strange; they exhibit mathematical figures, circles, triangles, and parallelograms, such as we find in no other plants, and their surface is often most elaborately sculptured. *Isthmia obliquata* here figured, is found in spring and early summer on the stems of many of the filiform Algæ, where it forms little glittering tufts a line or two in height. It has been brought from many distant parts of the world, both of the Atlantic and Pacific Oceans.

* Ralfs on British Desmidieæ. London, 1848. Thirty-five coloured plates.

Many other species accompany it in our own and other seas. The *Licmophora,* or *Fan-bearer,* which we also figure, is one of the most beautiful of our native kinds, and is very common in April and May on the leaves of *Zostera,* as well as on many of the smaller Algæ. It is very generally distributed round the British coasts, forming gelatinous masses of a clear brown colour on the plants it frequents. Under the microscope, however, its colours are much more gay, a yellow shade, variously banded and marked with deeper coloured spots, tinging the fan-like leaves, which are borne on slender threads transparent as glass. The pieces or joints of which these plants are composed, are called *frustules;* and each frustule consists of a single cell, whose coat is composed of a very delicate membrane made of organized silex. That these plants have thus the power of withdrawing *silex,* or flint earth, in some manner from the waters of the sea, and fixing it in their tissues is certain, but the exact method in which this is effected has not been ascertained. A remarkable point in their history results from this power of feeding on flint. It is this:

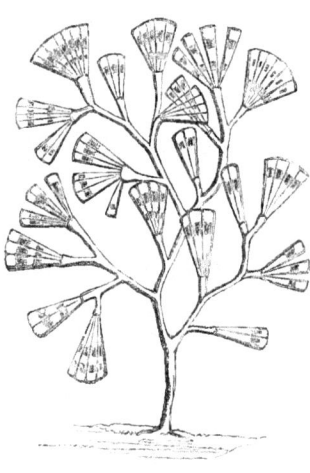

LICMOPHORA FLABELLATA.

their bodies are indestructible. Thus, their constantly accumulating remains are gradually deposited in strata, under the waters of the sea as well as in lakes and ponds. At first the effect produced by things so small—thousands of which might be contained in a drop, and millions packed together in a cubic inch, may appear of trifling moment, when speaking of so grand an operation as the deposition of submarine strata. But as each moment has its value in the measurement of time, to whatever extent of ages the succession may be prolonged, so each of these atoms has a definite relation to space, and their constant production and deposition will at length result in mountains. The examination of the most ancient of the stratified rocks, and of all others in the ascending scale, and the investigation of deposits now in course of formation, teach us that from the first dawn of animated nature up to the present hour this prolific family has never ceased its activity. England may boast that the sun never sets upon her empire, but here is an ocean realm whose subjects are literally more numerous than the sands of the sea. We cannot count them by millions simply, but by hundreds of thousands of millions. Indeed it is futile to speak of numbers in relation to things so uncountable. Extensive rocky strata, chains of hills, beds of marl, almost every description of soil, whether superficial or raised from a great depth, contain the remains of these little plants in greater or less abundance. Some great tracts of country are literally built up of their skeletons. No country is destitute of such monuments, and in some they constitute the leading features in the structure of the soil. The world is a vast catacomb of *Diatomaceæ;* nor is the growth of those old dwellers on our earth diminished in its latter days.

These earliest inhabitants of the world seem destined to outlive beings of larger growth, whose race has a definite limit, both ends of its existence comprised far within the duration of a species of *Diatomaceæ.* Many of the existing species are found in a fossil state, even in early beds. No part of our modern seas is without this ever-springing vegetation. Of this fact the late Antarctic Expedition* afforded many striking proofs. One of the objects of that expedition was to obtain soundings of the deep sea; and these were made at depths which would have engulfed Chimborazo in the abyss: yet the lead constantly brought up *Diatomaceæ*, even if nothing else. Nor did the eternal winter of the Antarctic Sea diminish the number of these vegetables. Other sea-plants ceased at Cockburn Island, in the low latitude of 64° S.; and thenceforward the *Diatomaceæ* formed the whole vegetation. The icy wall, called Victoria Barrier, which at length stopped the southward progress of the intrepid navigators, was found embrowned with them. Floating masses of ice, when melted, yielded them in millions. In many places they formed a scum on the surface of the icy sea. But perhaps the most remarkable fact observed, is the result of soundings continued for four hundred miles along the Victoria Barrier, where the existence of a bank, of unknown thickness, but at least of the extent of surface stated, was found composed almost wholly of skeletons of these microscopic vegetables. Nothing else came

* See Hooker's "Flora Antarctica," vol. ii.

up with the lead. Here, then, was a submarine deposit in process of formation equalling in extent any similar deposit of the earlier world. Such strata are doubtless in course of accumulation in most parts of the ocean, and may be observed on our own shores; but this Antarctic bank is the grandest example of the kind which has been carefully investigated by an able naturalist. But it is not only the sea and the land which yield the relics of these plants; the *Diatomaceæ* perform long journeys through the air! This remarkable fact rests on the authority of the accurate Darwin, who collected at sea small dust, which fell from the atmosphere on the planks and rigging of the ship, which dust, when examined with the microscope, was found composed of *Diatomaceæ*. These were on their flight from America to Africa. From their silicious nature they resist even the strong heat of volcanoes, and their remains are found thrown up in the pumice and dust from the crater. In fact, it is difficult to name a nook on the face of the earth, or in the depths of the sea, where they are wholly absent, either in a dead or living state; and their office in the general economy, besides affording food for the humbler members of the animal kingdom, seems to be the preparation of a soil for a higher class of vegetables. This they effect by the minute division of the silicious particles laid up in their tissues, and probably make this nearly insoluble earth more fit for assimilation by other plants. We must also suppose them endowed, like other vegetables, with the power of decomposing carbonic acid and liberating oxygen; and thus, in their countless myriads, exercising no mean place in the household of Nature. Like their mistress, these, her humblest servants, work in secret. We know not what we owe them. But continued, as their existence is, through all time, and dispersed, as they are, through every part of the world—even where the ice-bound sea is peopled by nothing else—we may rest assured that they do perform some work which renders them worthy the care of a Providence who creates nothing superfluous. I have spoken of the *Diatomaceæ* as vegetables. Ehrenberg and many other writers regard them as infusorial animals; and indeed they have been bandied about from the animal to the vegetable kingdom at various times, according to the views of different naturalists. Latterly the evidence seems to have preponderated on the vegetable side, especially since the brilliant discoveries of Mr. Thwaites,* communicated to a late meeting of the British Association, have shown that their fructification is precisely analogous to that of some of the lower Algæ, and that the fruit resembles a spore.

A similar mode of fruiting is now discovered among *Desmidieæ*, which were also classed with *Infusoria* by Ehrenberg, and of these a large number, in fruit, are figured in the work of Mr. Ralfs, before alluded to; but as they are natives of fresh water, it is out of place to enter on their history here. I may, however, remark, that the curious spiny bodies found fossilized in flint, which often pass for *Xanthidia*, are now proved to be only the spores of various genera of *Desmidieæ*, whose full-grown fronds are amazingly unlike the spore in form. The

* See Thw., in "An. Nat. Hist.," N. S. vol. i. p. 162, &c.

mode of forming fruit in both these families, *Desmidieæ* and *Diatomaceæ*, which is also the mode among undoubted Algæ, is by the coupling together of two cells or frustules, when a passage is gradually formed between them, through which the contents of one cell are discharged into the other, where a dense mass of granular matter collects, which at length solidifies into a spore and bursts through the walls of the cell. As such a process of reproduction is more analogous to what takes place in the vegetable than in the animal kingdom, naturalists seem now generally agreed to class them with vegetables. The advocates for their animal nature appeal to certain motions, having the character of voluntary motion, observed in many species. Thus *Bacillaria paradoxa* alternately propels its frustules forward and draws them back, opening out the filament of which the compound body consists into a straight line, and contracting it again into a narrow compass. This little plant resembles a pack of narrow cards, joined together at one of the angles of their smaller end: when extended they are ranged in a straight line, and when contracted they are folded back on each other and lie as if in a pack. It is highly curious to watch the regular manner in which this motion is continued. Some of the other species have movements of a similar character, but many have not been observed in motion: and such motions as are seen, more resemble the regulated movement of a machine than the voluntary changes of place which animals exhibit. No doubt it is difficult, perhaps impossible, to draw a rigid line between the irritability of a vegetable and the muscular and nervous contractions of an animal, when we come to investigate such minute organisms as those we are now considering; but it is, at least, certain that mere motion, such as has been observed in the *Diatomaceæ*, is no proof of animality. And as the other points in their history ally them to the vegetable kingdom, the fact of their vegetability, if not quite proved (as I believe it to be), is, at least extremely probable. I cannot enter in this place into the classification of these singular plants. The best account of the British species is to be found in several papers communicated by Mr. Ralfs to the Botanical Society of Edinburgh, and published in the " Annals of Natural History," in which figures of many species are given. Figures of a few others have appeared in " English Botany," and in " Grev. Crypt. Scot. ;" but a general history of the group remains a desideratum, which, it is to be hoped, Mr. Ralfs or Mr. Thwaites—perhaps the only persons in Britain capable of doing full justice to the subject—will favour us with. Both genera and species are extremely numerous, and, no doubt, great numbers await, in our waters, the eye of the naturalist, ready to reward him for his pains with a rich harvest of novelty and beauty.

Before dismissing the subject of microscopic vegetables, I may remark that the colouring of the waters of the Red Sea is now generally supposed to be caused by the presence of countless multitudes of a minute Alga, which is perfectly invisible to the naked eye, except when great numbers are congregated together. Some writers have denied that the water of the Red Sea has any peculiar colour, or that its name is owing to the colour of its waters. Others, on the contrary, describe a red shade, of a very singular character, as present, and various explanations of the phenomena have been given. The differences among travellers in their account of this sea may be reconciled by supposing their observations to have been made at different seasons of the year; for if the colour of the water depends on the presence of vegetable matter, it is highly probable that it will vary in degree at different seasons. That its waters are occasionally coated with a scum of a red colour is certain; and portions of it have been brought home and carefully examined by several naturalists. M. Montagne has given an elaborate account of specimens which he had received, and has proved that the scum is entirely made up of a very minute Alga, which consists of delicate threads, collected in bundles, and contains rings of a red matter, within a slender tube. This little plant has a structure very similar to the *Oscillatoriæ*, which form green scums on stagnant pools; or perhaps it more nearly resembles the pretty little fresh-water Alga, called (by the somewhat jaw-breaking name of) *Aphanizomenon*. Minute Algæ of this description are by no means confined to the waters of the Red Sea, but are met with in many parts of the ocean, sometimes extending in broad bands for hundreds of miles. Mr. Darwin, in his interesting voyage, gives an account of several extraordinary bands of this description which he met with in the Pacific Ocean. I have had the advantage of inspecting some of the specimens brought home by this naturalist. They are very similar to the species of the Red Sea.

Along the margin of the tide, as well as at different levels of the sandy beach, and in the crevices of rock-pools, may frequently be seen small patches of drifted sand and shells, the examination of which will often afford the patient explorer a rich treat. Broken shells and fragments of Zoophytes may compose a considerable portion of the drift, but a careful examination with a lens will generally detect a multitude of minute shells, some of them of very strange shapes, and others, structures of great elegance. The most singular of these minute shells are the *débris* of a curious tribe of animals, of low organization, called *Foraminifera*, all the species of which are of microscopic size. One genus of this tribe, called *Lagena*, has a shell resembling either a modern flask, or an ancient amphora or bottle, so perfectly that one might suppose the artist had taken the minute shell for his model. There are several species and varieties found in drift-sand, and most of these exist in a semi-fossilized state in the sands of ancient beaches. A monograph of the British species has been given by Mr. W. C. Williamson,*

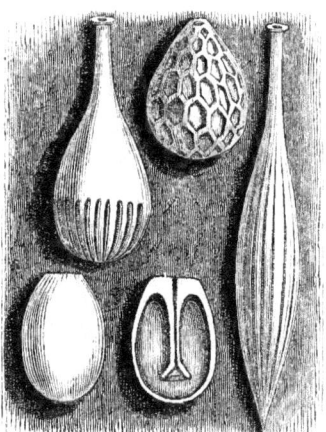

LAGENA.

* "Annals of Nat. Hist.," 2nd Series, vol. i. (1848) p. 1, &c.

from whose beautiful figures our cut has been copied. Mr. Williamson reduces the British species to eight, and disposes them under two groups, *Lagena* proper, distinguished by having the oral extremity of the flask produced into an external tubular neck ; and *Entosolenia*, characterised by an internal tube, rising from the upper extremity of the shell, and prolonged downwards into its cavity; as if the neck, instead of being prolonged from the body, were introverted. Four species of each genus are described. The shells of other *Foraminifera* are of a more complex structure, consisting of a number of distinct chambers, arranged one after another, like those of a Nautilus, communicating with each other by pores, and variously disposed, either in a spiral order or in straight or curved lines. There are many species, placed in several genera, found on the British coasts. Two of the commonest species are represented in our figure. Both may be found in a dead state in the fine shelly drift-sand, and living specimens may often be seen attached to the stems of various small Algæ. Such structures as these curiously imitate the chambered shells of the Nautili, and still more strikingly resemble, in miniature, the fossil remains of an earlier world. Their resemblance to the Ammonites, in particular, caused them, at one time, to be referred to a similar class of beings ; and their minute size was regarded as characteristic of a worn-out

ROTALIA BECCARII AND POLYSTOMELLA CRISPA.

type, consequent on an altered condition in the temperature and constituents of the sea. But an investigation of the animals of such species as have been found in a living state, has led to a great degradation in their position; and instead of being placed at the top of the class Mollusca, we now find them occupying a very humble station among Polypes. According to Dujardin, who has well examined into their history, the animal, in the *Foraminifera*, is absolutely deprived of distinct organs of locomotion, and even of respiration, being composed of a succession of joints or lobes, which go on increasing successively, and enveloping each other. It is coated by a shell, variously formed in different genera, but having a common character in being pierced with innumerable minute holes or pores, by which the contained fleshy parts keep up a connexion with the water. The only time when the soft parts of the animal are visible externally, is when a new joint is produced which has not completed the formation of its shelly chamber. On breaking the shell, the composition of the soft parts of the animal is found to be as simple and of as low organization as in the Hydra, or any other of the less complex Polypes; and if the shelly parts be dissolved in a mixture of alcohol and weak nitric acid, the body may be extracted entire, and will be found to consist of a series of articulations, filling up the several chambers of the shell. The various genera of *Foraminifera* are not characteristic of the modern ocean merely, but existed in former periods, and are found in geological deposits of various ages. Nor do they seem to have degenerated in size, the species of early date being no bigger than those now existing. Their resemblance to Nautili and Ammonites is merely one of analogy.

Drift-sand should also be closely examined for shells of the more minute Gasteropodous Mollusca. A wonderful variety of minute spiral univalve shells is found on our shores; though they are scarcely of so small a size as to come within the list of genuine microscopic objects. A simple pocket lens is sufficient to ascertain the characters of most. The different kinds of *Rissoa*, formerly included in the multifarious genus *Turbo*, are elegant little shells, whose spiral coils are variously sculptured or ribbed, sometimes in a very elaborate manner. Mr. Alder* has figured and described a considerable number of these small shells, many of them collected from drift-sand. Others may be obtained by the gatherers of sea-weeds with little trouble, if they will only preserve the sediment that collects in the water in which their sea-weeds are washed. The *Rissoæ* are vegetable-feeders, and live among the branches of the smaller sea-weeds, which are sometimes found as thickly covered with them as bushes are with snails. When the sea-weeds are plunged into fresh-water, the *Rissoæ* are quickly killed and fall to the bottom, and may then be secured by simply straining the water through a piece of canvas. Many other minute and curious animals, and sometimes Diatomaceæ, may be collected in a similar way.

Among the animated wonders of the sea, though not all of microscopic size, few tribes are more singular in structure and in their history, or more beautiful in their varied forms, than the *Acalephæ*, or Jelly-fishes, to whose

* "Annals Nat. Hist.," 1st Series.

phosphorescence the luminosity of the sea is chiefly attributable. Many of these creatures are of strictly microscopic size, and so transparent that they can scarcely be seen in the water in which they swim, except when revealed by the motion of their cilia or the flashes of light which they send forth in the dark; others are of comparatively large size, and some are even three or four feet in length. The sea in all climates produces these simple creatures, and sometimes swarms with them in countless multitudes. Even on our own coasts I have seen the shore rendered offensive for miles in extent by the stranding of shoals of minute *Medusæ*, each of which individually was scarcely bigger than a pea. But it is in tropical latitudes, and through the scarcely fathomable waters of the deep sea, that animals of this class display the greatest variety of form, and multiply in the greatest profusion. Here, too, the luminous species are of the largest size, and most brilliantly phosphorescent. Coleridge's description in the "Ancient Mariner" may convey some notion of their singular beauty :—

> " Beyond the shadow of the ship
> I watched the water snakes:
> They moved in tracks of shining white,
> And when they reared, the elfish light
> Fell off in hoary flakes.
> " Within the shadow of the ship
> I watched their rich attire:
> Blue, glossy-green, and velvet black
> They coiled and swam; and every track
> Was a flash of golden fire."

But it is difficult, in the most glowing description to convey an idea of the extraordinary effects produced by the presence of such countless luminous points scattered through the waters of the ocean. Sometimes the whole surface, far as the eye can stretch, seems one sheet of phosphorescent sheen; while looking down into the water close to the ship large globes of fire are seen slowly moving along at various depths. The wake of the vessel, at the same time, displays the most vivid and varied scintillations, and the spray that breaks on her prow falls off like a shower of many-coloured sparks. One scarcely knows on which part of this wonderful display of fireworks to fix the attention. One after another attracts our gaze, and in its turn appears most beautiful. The phosphorescence is not constant; it is most vivid when the water is disturbed. Thus the passing of the vessel causes an illumination, long continued in the wake she leaves behind : while a sudden breeze sweeping over the surface will send a stream of light far across the sea, strikingly similar to the dartings of the aurora through the realms of air. Such are some of the glories that the tropical ocean presents to us ; similar, but less brilliant illuminations are witnessed on our coasts, especially in warm evenings towards the close of summer, at which season vast multitudes of small *Medusæ* frequently swim along the shore, entering into creeks and bays, and sometimes literally converting the shallower inlets into strata of living jelly. At ordinary times many beautiful kinds may be collected by dragging a small gauze net after the boat, just below the surface of the water. In calm weather these little creatures rise to the upper strata of water, and sink again when the sea is troubled.

In structure, the *Acalephæ* or Jelly-fishes are exceedingly simple, but not the less wonderful on that account. Our wonder is, indeed, the more excited when we find creatures of large size, as many of the *Medusæ* are, and endowed with considerable powers of perception and some strength and agility, formed of a few delicate tissues filled with a fluid, to all appearance, not very different from sea-water. It is as if we had to investigate the structure of submarine bubbles. Take one of the largest of the race, weighing many pounds while living, and dry it. The whole contents of the body will either leak away or evaporate, and nothing will be left but some small shreds of membranous skin, forming a glistering stain on the surface of whatever object the Jelly-fish was placed upon. The flesh is entirely composed of large cells of delicate structure, filled with a transparent fluid. But these cells are put together with the most rigid accuracy, and their arrangement is so varied that naturalists have had to distinguish numerous families and genera of Jelly-fishes. The number four prevails through the whole class. All the parts of the body are divisible by four, and mostly ranged in a radiate manner round a centre, so that either the animal is cruciform, or its internal parts are so arranged. But this form, though very general, is not universal :—some resemble long ribbons ; others are oval or irregularly curved.

The Jelly-fishes have been classed according to differences in their locomotive organs. Our most common species, referable to the Linnæan genus *Medusa* (but now comprising several distinct genera, according to the views of modern naturalists), are distinguished by an umbrella-shaped body, generally pellucid, from the centre of which on the concave side depends a cluster of variously fringed and lobed vessels, which constitute the digestive system of the animal, while numerous slender fibres or tentacula hang from the border of the umbrella-shaped disc. Such a creature resembles an animated mushroom, with its gills and stalk. Sometimes the stalk is reduced to a minute point, and there are very many modifications. The motion in all Jelly-fishes of this shape is accomplished by alternate contractions and expansions of the umbrella, repeated at regular intervals, something like the movement of the lungs in respiration, in allusion to which resemblance this order of Jelly-fishes has been called *Pulmonigrade.* The convex end of the umbrella is directed forwards, the fimbriated vessels and tentacula stream behind, and the creature is propelled with a steady and graceful motion, very rapid in some species. Unsightly and repulsive as the Jelly-fish looks when stranded and lying exposed among sea-wrack on shore, it is a most beautiful animal when expanded in its native element and moving along in freedom. Nor is it so defenceless as its low organization and the softness of its parts may lead us to suppose. Many of the species are capable of inflicting a sharp and painful sting, sufficiently strong to paralyse the animals on which they prey, or perhaps to ward off danger when attacked by superior foes; while the long tentacles with which most of them are furnished are admirably adapted for seizing prey, as they adhere to whatever comes within their reach. A complete work on British *Medusæ* is still a desideratum, but the task has been commenced by Professor Edw. Forbes, whose beautifully illustrated history of the Naked-eyed *Medusæ* is a model for future observers.

The Jelly-fishes of another order called *Ciliograde*, move from place to place by means of innumerable vibratile hair-like organs, called *cilia*, variously disposed on the surface of their body. The common *Beroe* of our shores offers a charming example of this sort of motion. This little creature is met with in summer on most parts of the coast, swimming near the surface, and may readily be taken in a gauze drag-net. It has a melon-shaped body, from half an inch to nearly an inch in length, clear as crystal, and divided as it were into gores by eight longitudinal equidistant bands or ribs. These ribs when minutely examined are found clothed with innumerable flat plates, resembling the paddles of a water-wheel, placed one above another, and acting under the control of the will of the animal. When the Beroe wishes to move, these paddles are set in motion, and by their united action on the water propel the living globe of crystal with a swift and easy motion, forwards or backwards as it wills; and when it wishes to turn, it merely stops the movement of its paddles on one side. The cilia, in sunlight, reflect brilliant prismatic colours, and in darkness flash with a beautiful blue light. Delicate as are its organs of motion, the fishing apparatus of the Beroe is not less elegant. This consists of two long and exceedingly slender tentacula, five or six inches in length when fully extended, but capable of being wholly withdrawn within the body of the creature, where they are lodged in tubular sheaths. To the long filament is attached, at regular distances, a multitude of shorter and much more slender fibres, which are coiled up in spirals when the main filament contracts, and gradually spread out as it lengthens. These are very similar to the small hooked threads attached at intervals along a fishing-line. The Beroe may be kept alive for some time in a large vessel of sea-water, but it soon languishes, and melts away to nothing.

A third order of Jelly-fishes is called *Physograde*. In these the body is buoyed up by a sort of bladder, which the creature is said to have the power of inflating at will, so as to be able to rise or sink at its pleasure. The best known of this group is the *Physalia*, or Portuguese man-of-war, common in the seas of warm countries, but very rarely captured on the British coasts. Occasionally it is met with on the southern shores of

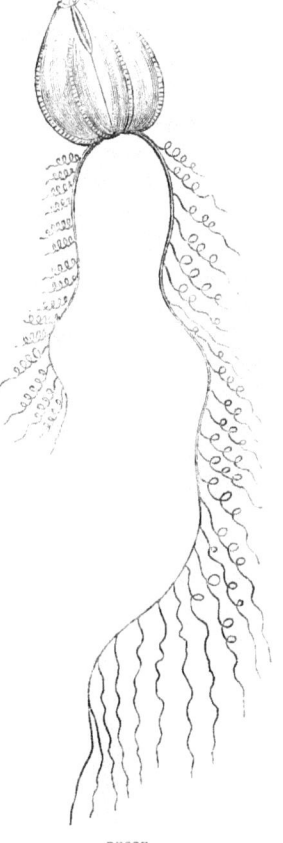

BEROE.

England and Ireland. It is, notwithstanding a somewhat grotesque form, a most lovely animal. The floating bladder is nearly egg-shaped, with a sort of snout at one end, and a pointed tail at the other, and crested with a crenate ridge of fine purple. The surface is glassy, and reflects all the colours of the rainbow. From the lower side of this singular organ depend a great number of tubular filaments, of various lengths and shapes; some of them cylindrical, others wavy and tapering to a point, and others resembling fine threads of chenile spirally convoluted; the whole, too, is gay with brilliant changeable tints of green, blue, and gold. These are the organs of prehension, absorption, and digestion, in fact of all the animal powers bestowed on the creature, and they are suffered to play freely in the nourishing element. Beautiful as the Physalia is, it is merely a system of entrails floating with the waves.

The *Cirrhigrade* Jelly-fishes present us with rather a higher type of structure. In these we have something like a skeleton, surrounded by the soft substance of the body. The *Velella*, which sails on the surface of the sea, and is brought in such numbers to our western and southern shores in the summer and autumn, furnishes an example of this order. It has an oblong-flattish body, between membranous and fleshy, transparent, but clouded with thickly-set dots of dark-blue, and containing within its substance a rectangular, boat-shaped, membranous skeleton, concentrically striate, and furnished with a vertical plate, placed diagonally, transparent, and of a horny membranous texture. The internal skeleton is of an exceedingly light and spongy nature,

THE VELELLA. 191

filled with air-cells and sufficiently buoyant to keep the animal on a level with the surface of the water; and the vertical plate, rising into the air, acts like a sail, by

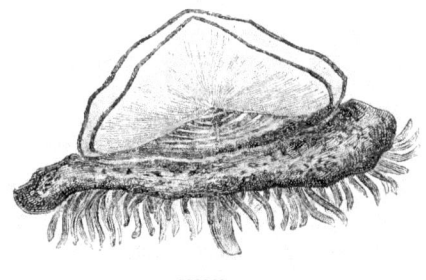

VELELLA.

which the creature is driven rapidly along. From the lower surface of the body hang down numerous long, dark-blue, tentacular appendages, or *cirrhi*, disposed in several rows, by the motion of which the animal can change its direction, or move along when there is not wind enough to catch its tiny sail. It is a fearless navigator, boldly venturing,

"Like little wanton boys, that swim on bladders,"

across the widest and deepest ocean. Perhaps none of the Jelly-fishes have a more extended geographical range. Their centre appears to be in the warmer parts of the ocean, and they are sent northwards and southwards into high latitudes of either hemisphere by the force of the great oceanic currents. On the west coast of Ireland, especially towards the close of the summer, vast numbers of *Velellæ* are driven on shore, entangled in floating sea-weed, and very frequently accompanied by the beautiful *Ianthina*, or "Blue Snail-shell," a singular Mollusc that equally "swims on bladders." In the *Velella* of our shores the sail is immoveable, and the vessel is therefore much at the mercy of the winds, but there is an exotic species which is said to have the power, by the contraction of muscular bands, to lower its sail at pleasure.

Many circumstances in the history of the ACALEPHÆ are calculated to excite curiosity or admiration, but, perhaps, there is no fact connected with them more wonderful than the mode of their reproduction from *gemmæ* or buds. It is a character of the vegetable kingdom, that its organisms propagate themselves in two ways: one by seeds, formed by special organs called flowers; the other by gemmæ or buds, which may be developed from any part of the cellular substance of the plant. Both modes of reproduction effect a similar object,—the continuance of the species: —but it is observable that individual characters are more strictly perpetuated when plants are multiplied by buds than when they are grown from seeds; hence, one mode of growth is said to be a multiplication of the individual plant, the other, a propagation of the species through new individuals. In the higher classes of animals propagation by gemmæ does not occur: the young are brought forth either in a fully-formed state, or in eggs, from which they will in time be hatched. As we descend lower in the series we find the process considerably varied, and become familiarized with certain transformations through which the young creature passes

METAMORPHOSES. 193

before it acquires its full complement of limbs. Even before we take leave of the Vertebrates, there are extraordinary examples of such transformations. Thus in the race of Frogs: the young, or tadpole, is deficient in limbs, swims like a fish, and breathes through gills; while the full-grown animal is, as every one knows, furnished with nimble and well-formed legs, and breathes through lungs. One can scarcely conceive a greater change in organization than is here displayed before our eyes. It strikes us as wonderful, because the young of other Vertebrates exhibit no such change after birth; and yet it would appear, from the researches of anatomists, that before birth the fœtus of all, not excepting that of man himself, undergoes changes of an analogous nature. So that here, as everywhere, Nature vindicates her uniformity. All of the vertebrate class are destined to go through a certain round of changes, but in some a portion of these changes take place before birth, in others after it.

Leaving the Vertebrates, in which transformation of the young after birth is the exception, we reach the Articulate or Insect races, in which it becomes the rule. All are familiar with the quadruple state under which insect-life appears,— the egg, the grub or caterpillar, the chrysalis, and the perfectly-formed insect. In these, as in the Frog, we find the young animal fitted for a condition of life totally different from that to which its mature state is destined; and, in many cases, the difference in its breathing apparatus is equally great. The young of many insects, as of the Dragon-flies and Gnats, live under water until their last change, when,

o

rising to the surface, they cast aside their skin, with its gills and fins, and thenceforward breathe the air through which they fly. Similar changes we have already noticed in the Crustacea, and such we may have to speak of in other classes of animals, but these are not of the same nature as what we have now to describe as taking place in the ACALEPHÆ, or Jelly-fishes. The insect deposits an egg, and each egg will, in due time, produce an insect similar to its parent, and nothing more. But the Jelly-fish throws off organized bodies, which can scarcely be called eggs, but which may more justly be compared to the *gemmæ* or buds of a plant; for, from every one of them may spring a whole colony of Jelly-fishes. The extraordinary history of these creatures was first ascertained by M. Sars, a celebrated Swedish Naturalist. The English reader may find a more detailed account than is here given in Steenstrup's "Alternation of Generations," published by the Ray Society, and in a very interesting memoir by Dr. Reid in Taylor's "Annals." *

Without adopting all the theoretical inferences deduced from the "alternation of generations," we may state the facts as follows. The Medusa gives birth to a multitude of minute gelatinous bodies, in shape not very unlike the so-called eggs of a sponge, or the spores of one of the lower Algæ, and, like them, furnished with a multitude of *cilia*, or vibratile hairs, which clothe the surface, and by their motion propel the little body through the water. These active little bodies must, I think, be looked upon as gemmæ or buds, rather

* " An. Nat. Hist." (1848), p. 25, &c. See also Forbes's " Monograph of the British Naked Eyed Medusæ, Ray Society," 1848.

than as young Medusæ, properly so called. When emitted, the bud is of an oval shape, broader at one end; and it constantly keeps its broader end in advance when moving. Internally they present a cavity. They are at this stage bags of living jelly, clothed with vibratile hairs. After a while the *bud* attaches itself by its larger extremity, or apparent front, to any convenient object,—as a stone or the stalk of one of the larger sea-weeds,—and this extremity henceforward becomes the base on which all its future operations are conducted. When it has become fixed by this base an alteration of form quickly commences. The body lengthens, and becomes wider upwards; and, at its upper extremity, is formed a mouth, which at first, is of small size and naked, but gradually becomes larger and surrounded by four prominences. These prominences soon increase in length, and change into long slender *tentacula* or feelers. After a few days new tentacula make their appearance between the old ones, and these organs, developed successively, one set after the other, are gradually increased to the number of twenty-eight or thirty. We have now the appearance of an animal resembling one of the more simple Polypes, such as the Hydra,—a bell-shaped, gelatinous, bag-like body, fixed to a stalk, highly contractile in every part, and furnished with a mouth surrounded by tentacula.

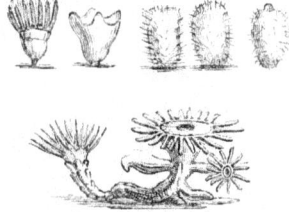

MEDUSÆ-BUDS IN VARIOUS STAGES.

At this stage, if we omit the stalk, there is no very remarkable dissimilarity to the parent Medusa. Like it, this has a capacious stomach, with strong powers of digestion and a voracious appetite. But the little creature soon exhibits characters which in the animal kingdom can be compared only to the growth of the compound Polypes, and which closely resemble the developement of plants from buds, or of the lower classes of cryptogamic plants from their spores. The lower part of the Medusa-bud throws out branches, or *stolons*, and these form new buds; or, buds may rise from any parts of the surface of the parent one, though it is more usual for them to spring from the lower part. When the powers of life are active, several of these secondary buds grow at the same time. They make their appearance as prominences, and gradually increase in size. As each enlarges, its apex pushes out, and curves downwards till it reaches an object to which it can attach itself. The apex having thus attached itself becomes the base, and the former base by which the bud was connected with the parent-bud separates, and is changed into the apex, in which a mouth, gradually surrounded with tentacula, is formed. And thus from a single bud a multitude of new buds, each endowed with similarly prolific powers, are developed. Nor does there seem any fixed period at which this system of growth by budding necessarily ceases. Dr. Reid kept some "colonies" of these buds for upwards of seventeen months before any material change in habit was observed to take place. During all this time stolons and buds continued to be formed and to die, but still the colony increased in numbers. It is probable, however, that the long continuance in the state of buds was owing to artificial confinement, and that in freedom the buds regularly develope perfect Medusæ in their season.

The mode in which perfect Medusæ arise from the buds is not the least remarkable phase of this singular history. When a bud has reached a proper size it becomes cylindrical, elongated, and much diminished in diameter. At this stage transverse wrinkles begin to appear at regular intervals, commencing near the top, and gradually extending downwards. As the operation proceeds, the uppermost wrinkles become deeper, dividing the body into ring-like segments. The tentacula gradually waste away, and the uppermost ring acquires a border formed of eight equidistant lobes or rays. This process goes on: ring after ring is bordered with rays, and these rings begin gradually to separate at the edges, till the upper portion of the cylinder resembles a number of shallow cups, piled one in another. As the furrows between them become deeper, the rings acquire greater powers of mobility, and at length an independent life is developed in each. The uppermost segment falls off, and immediately assumes the swimming habits of a young Medusa, but is only gradually moulded to its perfect form. The next segment follows:—and thus the cylinder continues to form and to

YOUNG OF MEDUSÆ FORMING.

throw off, one after another, the little creatures destined henceforth to act according to their " own sweet will," and in their proper season to produce new germs or buds, from which other young Medusæ shall arise. During this process of throwing off young Medusæ in the upper part of the column, its lower part continues to grow, and to become ringed as it grows; and Dr. Reid counted on a single column thirty or forty rings thus in process of conversion at the same time. Nor is this all: the same accurate observer assures us, that in no case does the formation of rings continue to the base of the column; but that after a time the ringing process ceases; the stump which remains throws out tentacula from its apex, and continues to live as a bud, ready, it would appear, either to form new stolons, or buds, or to resume the functions of a parent, and throw off a new batch of young ones. The whole is so similar to what takes place in the vegetable kingdom, where a season of rest follows the season of blossoms, that we are tempted to suppose a somewhat closer connexion than one of mere analogy between the two operations. Among animals the facts now stated are by no means isolated. A very similar mode of growth and propagation is found among the compound Polypes, whose gemmules, like those of the Medusæ, are at first free, and moved by cilia; afterwards attached, and budding forth with a plant-like body. And, omitting differences of organization, the great difference which strikes us in the process is, that in the Polype the fully developed animal continues throughout its life attached to the trunk, or *polypidom;* while in the Medusæ the young becomes detached at an early age, and continues to increase in bulk, and reaches maturity by its unassisted powers.

Perhaps a more extraordinary instance of "alternation of generation," and one in which the idea conveyed in that term seems to be most fully brought out, occurs in the genus *Salpa*, one of the Ascidians. In a former chapter I noticed some of the more common forms of this family, some of which, it will be remembered, are simple animals; others compound, or living in indissoluble association, organically connected one with another. Now the *Salpa* is a genus of this family which, in alternate generations, exhibits the character of a simple or of a compound Ascidian.

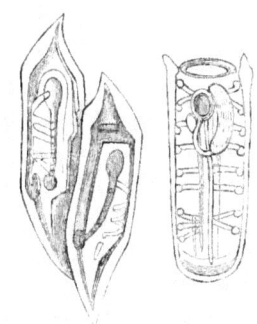

SALPA RUNCINATA, IN ITS FREE AND ASSOCIATED STATES.

That is to say, a compound *Salpa* produces simple young, and a simple *Salpa* compound young. The nature of this change will be more evident when I have described the appearance of the animal in both phases of existence. The *Salpæ* are at all times free, swimming from place to place, and generally in flocks, through the waters of the ocean. Each animal resembles a tube; clear as crystal, through whose walls the coloured internal parts may be distinctly seen. Sometimes these animals are found solitary; at other times linked together in long chains, composed of many similar individuals. These chains glide through the waters with a regular serpentine movement, as if a common will influenced them; and yet every animal of the chain is a distinct individual, and capable of a separate existence, if the rules of the brotherhood be dissolved. While swimming in the water, the chain appears like a single animal; but when taken up it falls to pieces, and the animals of which it is composed have no further power to unite: yet they can continue to exist. But this is not the wonderful part of their history. The strange fact connected with them is this, that the animals chained together only represent one phase of *Salpa* life. There are other individuals, of the same species, but of a very different form, which have never been united in chains, but have at all times lived solitary. And still more strange, these solitary *Salpæ* are the young of *Salpæ* that have been chained; and the progeny of these solitary ones will be chained *Salpæ*. Nay, it has been ascertained to be an invariable fact that the ovum of one of the chained *Salpæ* produces a solitary animal, while the ovum of a solitary *Salpa* produces a chain. Or, as Chamisso, who first observed this peculiarity, graphically says, "A *Salpa*-mother is not like its daughter, or its own mother, but resembles its sister, its grand-daughter, and its grand-mother." Our figure, copied from Professor E. Forbes, represents both states of the only recorded British species.

In Steenstrup's Memoir, already alluded to, the various aspects of these alternate developements have been ably discussed; and the Author has, I think, clearly established his position that even metamorphoses so unexpected as these, are not at variance with the harmony of Nature, but are really instances and further manifestations of that harmony. His object is to show that, under some modification or other, they exist in all classes of animals below the Vertebrates. The wellknown circumstances in the history of *Aphides*, and the existence of numerous sexes of bees, wasps, and ants, each having its assigned office, have been skilfully compared with the facts we have just been discussing, and an unexpected connexion established among them. It is thus one department of Nature throws light upon another, proving that to understand any part it is necessary to be acquainted with more. And this consideration ought to cure us of making rash assertions as to what is or is not possible in a natural phenomenon. When Chamisso first announced his discovery of the propagation of *Salpæ*, he was laughed at as a dreamer. And now, not only is the fact, as described by Chamisso, established in its minutest details, but it is shown to be by no means isolated, and it receives support and confirmation from the most unexpected quarters.

> Now is it pleasant in the summer-eve,
> When a broad shore retiring waters leave,
> Awhile to wait upon the firm fair sand,
> When all is calm at sea, all still at land;
> And there the ocean's produce to explore,
> As floating by, or rolling on the shore;
> Those living jellies which the flesh inflame,
> Fierce as a nettle, and from that their name ;
> Some in huge masses, some that you may bring
> In the small compass of a lady's ring ;

Figured by Hand Divine—there 's not a gem
Wrought by man's art to be compared to them ;
Soft, brilliant, tender, through the wave they glow,
And make the moonbeam brighter where they flow,
Involved in sea-wrack, here you find a race,
Which science doubting, knows not where to place ;
On shell or stone is dropped the embryo seed,
And quickly vegetates a vital breed.
 While thus with pleasing wonder you inspect
Treasures, the vulgar in their scorn reject,
See as they float along th' entangled weeds
Slowly approach, upborne on bladdery beads ;
Wait till they land, and you shall then behold
The fiery sparks those tangled fronds infold,
Myriads of living points ; the unaided eye
Can but the fire and not the form descry.
And now your view upon the ocean turn,
And there the splendour of the waves discern ;
Cast but a stone, or strike them with an oar,
And you shall flames within the deep explore ;
Or scoop the stream phosphoric as you stand,
And the cold flames shall flash along your hand ;
When, lost in wonder, you shall walk and gaze
On weeds that sparkle, and on waves that blaze.
CRABBE.

GANNETS, PUFFINS, CORMORANTS, ETC.

CHAPTER VII.

SEA-SIDE PLANTS, BIRDS, DRIFTWOOD, ETC.

COAST scenery is so varied in its character that it is impossible to describe it, without localizing; and our plan prevents us from indicating any place. Nothing can be more dissimilar than the eastern and western shores of the British Islands, — the one flat, sandy, shingly, with few harbours, and a slightly indented coastline; the other rock-bound, with bluff headlands, abounding in harbours, and deep bays which penetrate far into the land, while all exposed places are lashed by the heavy swells of the Atlantic. A person who has seen the sea only on the east coast of England, can form but a feeble conception of that—

> ———— glorious mirror, where the Almighty form
> Glasses itself in tempests ; in all time
> Calm or convulsed—in breeze, or gale, or storm,
> Icing the pole, or in the torrid clime,
> Dark heaving ;—boundless, endless, and sublime.

The general colour of the water, and the play of light on the surface, are totally different on our eastern and western coasts. The greater depth, near land, on a rock-bound shore, and the different colour of the bottom, cause the waters on the west coast to have a deeper blue; and the absence of sand and mud give them greater clearness, so that it is not uncommon, in gliding along in a boat, to see below us sea-weeds waving and fishes swimming at a depth of many fathoms. But it is not merely in colour that the western ocean surpasses the sea on our eastern coasts. The broad Atlantic, free from impediment for a thousand leagues, breasts high against the rocks, and even in summer there is often a swell such as is seen only in the storms of winter elsewhere. These grand swells, clear as emerald, moving in with a slow and stately step, break in thunder on the rocks, throwing up glorious showers of spray : and this amid the sunshine of a summer's noon, when there is no wind, or only sufficient breeze from the land to throw back the top of the wave in a feathery crest, while the great mass of water, with arching neck, breaks in an opposite direction. Not that such occurs on every summer day : there are times when the ocean takes its rest. But these great breakers are the relics of some storm which has roused his strength a thousand miles away, and come to our peaceful coasts, like the rejoicings after victory, to tell of his power and majesty.

The aspect of the coast is thus indefinitely varied. There are, however, characters, which a naturalist will at once detect, common to most seashores. The vegetation, in general, has not the luxuriance which an inland situation affords. The trees are of smaller size, of slower growth, and apt to be bent by the prevalent winds, or their tops shorn by the salt air. On many coasts, trees will not grow beyond the shelter of walls or rocks, and forest-trees dwindle into stunted shrubs. Then there are numerous plants which are peculiar to the seashore, and which are never found far from the coast. I have already mentioned the Sea-reed (*Ammophila arundinacea*) which flourishes among drifting sands, and binds together the

HORNED POPPY.

mass with its matted roots. Still nearer to the beach, and even among the larger stones that border it, many gay-flowered plants are seen scattered about. The Yellow-horned Poppy (*Glaucium luteum*) and the Eringo (*Eringium maritimum*) are very characteristic of such a locality. The Horned Poppy forms a large crown of deeply-cut and very rough leaves, from which rise several straggling stems that lie along the ground, bearing here and there large yellow flowers, succeeded by horn-like pods, several inches in length. The Eringo is more erect, branching and bushy, and exceedingly rigid, with blue-green cut leaves, spinous like those of holly, and dense heads of small blue flowers. Several *cruciferous* plants, with flowers having four petals, forming a cross, and succeeded by long or short green pods, are peculiar to the sea-coast. One of these is the Sea-kail, well known in cultivation, but which may also be found on several sandy shores. Another is the Wild Cabbage (*Brassica oleracea*), supposed to be the origin of all the varieties of garden cabbage and greens, including cauliflower and brocoli in the list; these latter being monstrous states of the flowering branches. Wild Cabbage is particularly abundant under Dover cliffs, and all along that chalky shore; and in severe springs the young sprouts, which are earlier than those produced in gardens, are collected and brought to market. Some parts of the cliffs look precisely like cabbage-gardens. Another plant of this family, the Sea-rocket (*Cakile maritima*), with weak, smooth stems and rather succulent, pinnatifid leaves and purplish flowers, is common in sandy places. And two species of Stock (*Matthiola incana* and *M. sinuata*) are among the rarer species, the former being, perhaps, scarcely a genuine wild plant. Where the coast is muddy, another genus of this family *Cochlearia*, or Scurvy-grass, makes its appearance. Of this genus there are five British species, one of which is the Horse-radish. All cruciferous plants have anti-scorbutic qualities, and perhaps there is not any unwholesome plant in the order. Many are used for food, and all those that have soft and fleshy leaves and succulent roots, like the Turnip and Radish, are suitable for that purpose. The species are widely dispersed through temperate climates, but very rare in hot countries; and they are eight times more numerous in the northern than in the southern hemisphere. Many are now dispersed, through the agency of man, to every climate.

Salt-marshes near the coast have their peculiar vegetation. Coarse Sedges and Rushes grow in the wetter places, mixed with patches of *Aster*, whose purple flowers enliven the otherwise dreary and dismal scene. Various smaller plants are scattered in drier places. The Thrift or Sea-pink (*Armeria maritima*), and the different kinds of Sea-lavender (*Statice*) are peculiarly gay, growing wherever the mud becomes hardened. The former is not confined to such places, but often forms extensive patches or continuous soft cushions along the margin of the sea, and in May bears a profusion of its pretty pink flowers, which continue opening for the two following months. The Thrift is met with again on the summits of mountains, at a distance from the sea; but is not commonly found in intermediate places, except occasionally on the banks of large inland lakes. Some others of the plants of salt-marshes have a similar fancy for mountain air, particularly two kinds of Plantain (*Plantago maritima* and *P. coronopus*); and the chief difference which climate makes upon them is, that the leaves in the shore-grown plants are more succulent and contain a greater quantity of soda.

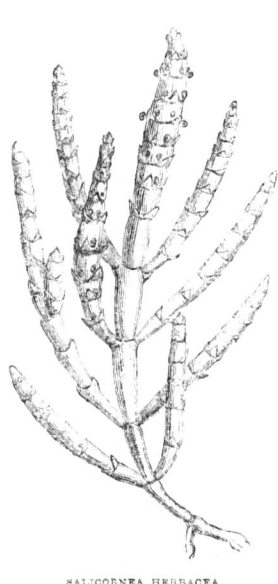

SALICORNEA HERBACEA.

One of the most characteristic plants of salt ground is the jointed Glass-wort (*Salicornea herbacea*), a small herb with fleshy stems, divided into joints, with minute flowers concealed in the axils of the scale-like leaves. This plant, like Samphire, is sometimes gathered for pickling; but it is rather an old-fashioned pickle, not often seen, even in country places. In the south of Europe, several others of the genus grow in great profusion, and are largely collected and burned for the sake of the soda contained in their ashes. The *Salicornia* belongs to the same family as the common weed called Goose-foot (*Chenopodium*); and others of its kind are natives of the coast; such as the various kinds of Orache (*Atriplex*), some of which are shrubby and not unornamental, and the Wild-beet (*Beta maritima*), whose leaves may be used as Spinach. The Spinach itself is one of the same tribe, many of which are used as esculents in various parts of the world. Some of them, such as the Garden Beet, or Mangold Wurzel ; and the *Chenopodium quinoa*, which is largely cultivated in Peru, are among the most important green crops in the countries where they flourish. Sometimes the Atriplices, particularly *A. portulacoides*, of our shores, grow in the pools of brackish water, or the drains made along a muddy shore, and then, not unfrequently, their stems may be found clothed with tufts of a delicate little sea-weed, *Bostrychia scorpioides*, the only one of the *Floridea* which is found in brackish water. It seems strange to find a genuine sea-weed growing upon the stems of a flowering plant.

GLAUX MARITIMA.

A common little shore-plant,*Glaux maritima*, placed by botanists in the same family as the Primrose, is interesting, not merely from its beauty, but from its imperfectly exhibiting the characters of the order. In the *Primulaceæ* there is generally a well-formed and large corolla, as is sufficiently obvious in the various kinds of Primrose, Auricula, and Polyanthus. In *Glaux* that organ is wholly wanting, but a coloured calyx supplies its place; in all other respects the little plant has the structure of the family. It has creeping stems which send up erect branches from two to six inches high, with small, oblong, fleshy leaves in whose axils small pink flowers are sessile. Each flower is five-cleft, and contains five stamens and one style. The Common Brook-weed (*Samolus Valerandi*), which grows in wet places, is another Primulaceous plant, interesting both from its structure and history. In form its flowers resemble very minute primroses, but have a row of rudimentary stamens alternate with the lobes of the corolla, and the sides of the ovary are united to the calyx. In both these characters it differs from other *Primulaceæ*. The point most curious in its history is that it is one of a small genus, whose species are found widely apart, and that it is itself a native not merely of the shores of Europe and America, but also of South Africa and New Holland. With the exception of *Cardamine hirsuta*, perhaps none of our wild-plants, that is not an absolute weed, has a wider range than *Samolus*. In places similar to where the *Glaux* is found, grow *Arenaria marina* and *rubra* (if they be distinct), small biennials with awl-shaped, opposite, fleshy leaves, and starry purple flowers that open in sunshine; each flower with five petals, ten stamens, and three styles. These little plants are associated by botanists with the Chickweed, and also with Pinks and Carnations in an order called *Caryophylleæ*. To the same order belongs the Catchfly (*Silene*), a species of which (*Silene maritima*), with bladdery calyces and smooth fleshy leaves, grows along the margin of the sea.

Sand-downs, where the herbage is close and thick, have often a very gay flora, composed of a great number of plants. The surface is generally carpeted with white clover, mixed with mosses, chiefly of the genus *Tortula* and small, fine-leaved grasses, especially *Nardus stricta* and some of the more wiry-leaved *Festucæ*, with here and there the characteristic Sand-reed. Such is the composition of the greensward which forms the groundwork of the piece. This is gaily ornamented with a profusion of the bright pink stars of Centaury (*Erythræa*), several kinds of which are distinguished. These are diminutive Gentians, with all the bitterness of foliage and brightness of flower peculiar to that family of plants. Among them may sometimes be seen their more ambitious brother the *Chlora*, with his golden eight-lobed crown; but this is rarely found except where there is limestone or chalk in the soil. Next we are attracted by different varieties of Wild Pansies (*Viola tricolor* and *V. lutea*), some of them blue, others yellow, and others a mixture of these colours with creamy white. Then Eye-bright, which, though diminutive, often indeed dwindled down to a pair or two of leaves and a pair of flowers, is still worthy both of its English name, and the more sounding Greek *Euphrasia*. Milkwort (*Polygala*), of three colours, white, blue, or red, abounds on such ground; as does also the singularly elegant *Asperula cynanchica*, whose hair-like stems, with narrow leaves in distant whorls support a branching tuft of white or pink tubular, four-cleft flowers. This graceful little plant is of the same family as the Madder (*Rubia*), and the Ladies' Bedstraw (*Galium*), and is still more closely connected with a greater favourite than either, the Woodruff (*Asperula odorata*). Several small species of Clover (*Trifolium*), some of them rare, are scattered about. One of the prettiest of these, though not rare, is *T. arvense*, or Hare's-foot Clover, a species with erect wiry stems, narrow leaves, and long cylindrical heads of flowers, clothed with soft silky hairs. These may be collected for the winter nosegay, the silky heads retaining their form and much of their colour in drying. Several wild Geraniums and Stork's-bills (*Erodium*) abound,—the long finely-cut leaves of the latter being more beautiful than the comparatively insignificant flowers. The more bare patches of sand are frequently diversified with scattered tufts of a half-shrubby Spurge (*Euphorbia paralias*), one or two feet high, with erect stems, clothed with closely-set, oblong, somewhat fleshy leaves, and bearing an umbel of greenish-yellow flowers. Like all the Spurges, it contains abundance of an acrid milky juice, which flows when any part of the stem or leaf is wounded. Most of the Spurges grow in similarly dry ground, in various parts of the world, and perhaps nowhere are they found of larger size or of stranger forms than in the burning sands of Africa. There the smooth stem, clothed with thin leaves, which marks our British kinds, is exchanged for a succulent stem, often destitute of leaves altogether, or having those organs converted into spines, or into lumpy bodies. The stem of some is columnar, rising into trees twenty to forty feet high, and bearing great naked branches like arms of gigantic candelabra; that of others is globose, or melon-shaped, armed with spiny ribs and furrows; and others again have a multitude of snake-like stems issuing from the expanded crown of their roots. In others the root itself forms the reservoir, being as large as a turnip or a beet; while an annual vegetation of soft leaves and flower-stalks is all that rises above the surface of the ground. All these varieties of habit are obviously designed to enable these plants to endure the climate and soil for which they are destined. Nourishment in some is stored up in the leaves, in others in the stem, and in others in the root, that they may have something to feed upon through the burning days and dewless nights of an African summer. Other plants contend with the difficulties of their situation by other means. Thus, one of the most beautiful of our native sand-hill plants, *Convolvulus Soldanella*, sends creeping stems under the surface of the sand in all directions, and these emit from the joints, or *nodes*, bundles of finely divided, hair-like roots, that penetrate the loose soil, and ramifying as they go along, are constantly forming mouths ready to suck up every drop of water that penetrates the sand. Besides this provision of abundant roots, its leaves, though less fleshy than in some plants, are so in some degree, and retain, in their tissues, moisture even in seasons of drought. Along the sandy shores of other countries, and throughout the tropics, are found species of Convolvulus related to our *C. Soldanella*, and these support existence by means of a similar system of creeping underground stems and fibrous roots. But with the soil the habit is varied; thus, in the arid plains of Persia, where probably a stiffer soil may prevent the spreading of underground stems, there are species of

Convolvulus forming thorny shrubs, not unlike our furze-bushes. It is singular to see such rigid and dry-looking sticks, yielding, in their season, flowers of the same structure and delicacy as the beautiful Bindweed of our hedges.

Rocky ground along the coast has its peculiar plants, but perhaps a less numerous list than that with which the sands supply us. Of course I omit a large number which are not confined to the shore, though they often mainly contribute to form some of the sweetest of the minute pictures that abound along the nooks and coves of the sea-coast. Primroses and Violets and Wild Thyme, are as abundant by the shore as they are in inland places, and so are Wild-roses. But there is one species of Rose, *Rosa spinosissima*, the origin of all the garden varieties of Scotch Roses, which is most abundant by the shore, growing either among rocks or on the sands. In the latter situation it is often extremely stunted, its stems not rising more than two or three inches above the surface, but even in that humble condition crowned with the large milk-white blossom of their kind. The leaves of this species are peculiarly small and neat, and its stems densely clothed with slender, spreading spines. On various parts of the English coast, especially in the south, different kinds of *Helianthemum*, or Rock-rose, cover maritime rocks, and are gay the whole summer with ever-renewing troops of white or yellow flowers, whose crumpled petals scarcely last a day. The stamens of these plants are sensitive. If the filaments be touched on the outside, near the base, the tuft will be seen gradually to open till they lie down in

GRASSY PASTURES NEAR THE SEA.

a circle distant from the pistil. The distribution of the British *Helianthema* is rather curious, from the scattered localities in which the several kinds occur. In Ireland there are only two species, one found but very sparingly in the south-west of Cork, the other confined to the Isle of Arran, on the Galway coast. In steep places by the sea, and especially on mural cliffs, the Tree-mallow (*Lavatera arborea*) is abundant in many places. This is the most woody of the British Mallows, forming an arborescent bush, six or eight feet high. But, notwithstanding its woody character it is only a biennial, and perishes after having once ripened fruit. The Tamarisk (*Tamarix*), though not common in a wild state, is well-known in gardens. It naturally grows by the sea-side, and is by much the most shrubby of the British coast-plants. Its long sprayey branches, clothed with minute leaves, and bearing late in autumn dense clusters of flesh-coloured flowers, are singularly elegant, as they wave to and fro in the breeze. We have but one native species ; but several others are found on the sea-shores of Europe and Asia, and some characteristic districts in the Steppes of Tartary, where these thin, twiggy shrubs alone relieve the widely-spread desolation and barrenness.

Grassy pastures near the sea are sometimes well stored with small bulbous plants, which dot them over with flowers, bright in their brief season. Early in spring the Vernal Squill (*Scilla verna*), and late in autumn the Autumnal (*S. autumnalis*), open their fairy stars of blue, on tiny scapes, an inch or two in height. These are common to many of our coasts. Another minute bulb

(*Trichonema Columnæ*), the smallest British species of the Iris family, occurs in one or two places* on the south coast of England, where it finds, perhaps, its most northern locality. It belongs to a genus whose species gradually increase in number and in gay clothing as you approach the sun, and which has its maximum at the Cape of Good Hope, where many sorts, with rich purple, golden, or milk-white flowers of large size, spangle the roadsides, or cover the barren ground near the sea with a many-coloured sheet. Several of the smaller *Orchideæ* are found in similar places, especially *Orchis morio*, whose dark purple flowers are among the first heralds of summer, and Lady's-tresses (*Spiranthes autumnalis*), which scents the grass in the hottest months.

In rambling thus along the shore, whether it be the bold headland, the sandy down, or the flat beach that engages our notice, plants are not the only objects that arrest the eye of a naturalist. Ever and anon his attention is attracted by the appearance of some bird, either one of the regular denizens of the coast, or a passing visitant. The birds which we meet with near the sea are so numerous, that (as I am not going to write a bird-history) I shall not notice them all, and those which I shall mention must be spoken of in a very cursory manner. Many that visit wooded shores belong more properly to woods and groves. The singing-birds are of this description, with the exception of the Lark, which frequents open pastures near the sea as much as those further inland, and may be heard pouring out his shrill melody above our heads through the live-long summer

* Dawlish Warren, Devonshire.

NATATORES, OR SWIMMING BIRDS.

day. Several, which in their habits are strictly landbirds, and never enter the water or feed on the products of the sea, pass their lives in its neighbourhood, and continually meet us on rocky coasts. Of these the Chough or Cornish Crow (*Fregilus graculus*) is one of the most remarkable. Its size is between that of a Rook and a Jackdaw, but it is more shapely than either, of a glossy blue-black colour, with bright red bill and legs. The bill is more slender than in others of the crow family, and is remarkably curved, and sharp-pointed. These birds build in inaccessible crags and cliffs along the coast, forming a nest of sticks, lined with wool and hair, in which are laid four or five yellowish-white spotted eggs. They feed on insects and berries, and sometimes on grain. Like others of the Crow tribe, they are easily tamed, if taken young, and exhibit in captivity the same restless curiosity and love of pilfering, and hiding what they steal, that mark the Raven and Jackdaw. Montagu has given us an interesting account of one of these birds which he kept for several years in his garden, and which became exceedingly bold and familiar. His account will be found copied into Yarrell's admirable "History,"—a source from which I have not scrupled to draw in the short notice that follows.

But the birds most characteristic of the coast belong to the groups of NATATORES, or Swimmers, distinguished by having webbed-feet, which act as paddles in propelling them through the water. This very extensive group contains numerous families, several of which are included in the British Fauna. At the head of the list

218 THE DUCK FAMILY.

are the *Anatidæ,* or Ducks and Geese; a family peculiarly characteristic of high latitudes, from which vast flocks annually migrate southwards, visiting our shores in the winter months. Some remain with us all the year, some only in the breeding-season, and others rarely show themselves, except when driven here, as into a harbour of refuge, in a severe season. The habits of many of this family are more lacustrine than littoral. They prefer inland pieces of water, fens, &c., nestling among the tall reeds and willows of the margin. But some are strictly littoral in their habits. One of the commonest of the latter is the Shell-drake (*Tadorna vulpanser*), a strikingly handsome species, with glossy-green head and neck, a white collar, and a body diversified with patches of chestnut, white and black; bright-red bill and flesh-coloured legs. The head is shorter and rounder than in the common duck, and the bill is remarkable for a prominence above, and a strong short hook at the extremity. The Shell-drake frequents sandy places near the coast, building in old rabbit-holes, and making its nest of grass, often ten or twelve feet distant from the entrance. This habit has in some places obtained for them the local name of Burrow-duck. Their commoner name is perhaps given from their being accustomed to feed on small mussels or other shell-fish; or, as Mr. Yarrell suggests, perhaps a corruption of *shield*-drake, because this bird is frequently introduced into heraldry. Very different in its colour, but somewhat similar in form, is the Scoter (*Odiemia nigra*), a common winter visitant. This bird has a uniformly black plumage, with black bill and legs. The head is shaped like that of the

Shell-drake, but the bill wants the strong hook at the extremity. It frequents the sea-shore in many places, often in considerable numbers, and feeds on small shell-fish and other molluscous animals. The flesh is oily, with a strong fishy taste, and thus "being identified with fish, it is allowed by the Romish Church to be eaten in Lent and on fast-days; and so great is the demand for it, that many devices are in use on the sea-coasts of [Roman] Catholic countries to obtain these ducks for the use of the table." * Mr. Yarrell, from

* The statement here given, on the authority of Mr. Yarrell, is, I have been recently informed, much too broad and unqualified. There is no *general* rule of the Roman Church on this subject, but in certain localities old customs of this nature have long prevailed, which are *permitted*, but not enjoined. That the Barnacle was formerly eaten in Ireland on fast days as fish, and that it may still be so used in some remote parts of the island, is a common opinion ; and a learned friend has pointed out to me a curious passage, to be found in an old Dutch book of travels in Europe, " Zeer gedenkwaardige en naankeurige historische Reis-beschrijvinge door Vrankrijk, Spangie, Italien, Duitsland, Engeland, Holland en Moscovien, p. 445," published at Leyden in 1700, of which there is a copy in the library of Trinity College, Dublin, to the following effect. Speaking of Ireland, the author says, " There are also many other animals, among which may be remarked a sort of bird out of the marshes, called Barnacles, which are produced in a wonderful manner. For they have neither father nor mother, nor come forth out of any eggs, but out of the gum of the fir-trees, which are common on the sea-shore. They are seen first to open the mouth, afterwards to move the body, and as soon as they feel themselves loose, fly into the air, or plunge into the water of the marshes. The clergy and ecclesiastics of the kingdom eat of these animals in the fasts, and give out that they are not produced from flesh of any kind." In making these remarks I wish distinctly to say, that nothing is farther from my thought, or would give me

whose work I make this extract, gives an interesting account of the stratagems employed for this purpose at places on the French coast, where the pursuit of this game is deemed so important as to be a matter of municipal regulation. At the end of the family of Ducks are placed the Mergansers, of which we have four British kinds. They differ chiefly from others of the family by the comparatively long and slender bill, furnished with fine teeth along the edges and hooked at the extremity. The form of their body resembles that of other Sea-ducks, and their habits are very similar. All our species are furnished with crests, or long feathers at the back of the head. The Smew (*Mergus albellus*), the smallest and commonest, is a very elegantly marked bird, white, diversified with black and grey; a black face, and slate-coloured bill, with a white neck and breast, and a white head, all but the face and poll-feathers,—the latter, forming the crest, being partly greenish-black and partly white. The Red-breasted Merganser (*Mergus serrator*) is a larger species, painted with equal variety, but in gayer colours. The head and throat are of a rich shining green, the neck white,

greater pain, than to wound the feelings of any member of the Church of Rome, in whose communion are included many friends whom I highly esteem, and one to whom I am bound by the closest ties of friendship. As to the matter in question, eating Barnacles as fish, we must bear in mind that at the time the custom originated, every one—including the naturalists of that day—firmly believed in the marine origin of this bird. To a later period—the Whale and Porpoise were supposed to be fishes — and if their flesh also had been eaten as fish, who would have questioned the propriety of the practice?

except a narrow dark line behind; at either side, before the wings, are numerous large white feathers, bordered by velvet-black; the lower part of the neck and breast is chestnut-brown, varied with dark streaks, and the body and wings are elegantly diversified with white, black, and brown feathers. The Goosander (*Mergus merganser*), our largest species, is found chiefly in the northern parts of the kingdom, whose shores it visits in winter. In its colours it somewhat resembles the last, having a dark-green head and throat; but the upper part of the body is more uniformly dark, and it wants the black-edged feathers in front of the wing, and, instead of the mottled breast, the lower part of the neck and under-surface of the body is a reddish-buff.

These Mergansers naturally lead us to the Grebes and Divers, or *Colymbidæ*, a family at once distinguished from the Duck tribe by the long conical bill, and the position of the legs, which are placed so far back, towards the tail, that when the bird leaves the water it stands nearly erect. The foot in the Grebes is only partially webbed, the toes being deeply divided, and merely winged with membrane; but in the Divers we find feet webbed like those of the Ducks. The Grebes have long beaks, and long bodies, but short wings, and an obsolete tail, and frequently long and dense feathers on the neck, forming a thick ruff round the throat. Their habits are more properly lacustrine than marine; they feed on small fish and aquatic insects, which they take by diving, pursuing their game under water with great agility. The little Dab-chick, so often seen in lakes and rivers, is the smallest and commonest of the genus, and its habits give a correct notion of those of the other species. The true Divers (*Colymbi*) most strongly exhibit the habits of the family. Of these the Great Northern Diver (*Colymbus glacialis*) is the largest, and, when fully grown, the handsomest; the upper part of the body being dark, elegantly spotted with transverse rows of white spots; the lower surface white; the head and neck black, with greenish tints, and two ring-like collars of mottled feathers. It is "a most expert and indefatigable diver, and remains down sometimes for several minutes, often swimming under water, and as it were flying with the velocity of an arrow through the air." It feeds on small fish, the shoals of which it follows along the coast, and captures its prey by diving after it. In the breeding-season these birds pass inland, and build their simple nest in some retired spot, on the borders of a lake or inlet. They are very shy at all times, and particularly at this season.

The family of *Alcadæ*, consisting of Guillemots, Auks, Razor-bills, and Puffins, contains several species that pass their lives in swimming and diving after fish, or in sitting perched on rocks in retired places of the coast. All these are birds of social habits, and congregate in vast flocks on the rocky islets and headlands of our northern and western coasts, where the pursuit of this game, either for the capture of the birds or their eggs, is conducted with the appliances more of savage than civilized life—the fowlers being suspended in mid-air by slender ropes from the cliff. In the form of the body these birds are very similar to the Divers;

the legs, which are short and thick, are inserted very far back, and give a still more erect carriage to the bird when on shore. The wings are short and small in proportion to the bulk of the body, and in one or two species so small as to be unfitted for flight. In this, and other respects, there is an obvious resemblance between this group and the Penguins of the southern hemisphere, in which the deficiency of wing, and fish-like motions and habits are carried to their greatest extent. The *Alcadæ* of the north may, indeed, be taken as the representatives of the Penguins (*Spheniscidæ*) of the south. The Common or Foolish Guillemot (*Uria troile*) is met with at all seasons. In breeding-time these birds congregate by hundreds and thousands on the rocks that they frequent, which, for the time, they and their associates convert into populous bird-cities. Nor are these bird-cities limited to single species. In May, when they begin to congregate, Guillemots, Auks, Razor-bills, and Puffins, as well as Gulls, visit the rocks in vast troops, and then begin such a hubbub and flutter that you would think there was going to be a fierce contest for the nesting-ground. But, after much debate, the matter is amicably settled, and the rock portioned out in ledges, one above another, to the different kinds. Here each lays its solitary egg, on the bare rock, or with very little protection; and on these eggs the birds sit, with fearless fidelity for the allotted time, in their peculiar erect posture. The name "foolish" is given to the Guillemots because, whilst hatching, they will rather suffer themselves to be taken by the hand than desert their change. A rock thus peopled from top to bottom with thousands of grave-looking birds, while others are soaring and screaming about them, is a very singular sight. The vast numbers of these birds surprise us, too, when we remember that each pair lays but a single egg. And such is also the case with the Penguins of the south, and with several other kinds of social birds. Nature has given them this limited power of multiplication, and has not exempted them from the usual number of enemies and accidents—and their enemies, besides man, are many—yet the race goes on still increasing. Is it their good temper or their stolidity that favours increase in this extraordinary degree? The young birds soon leave the rock, and, long before they can fly, are found swimming in the sea below, diving and catching fish like their parents. Fishermen assert* that the young Guillemot, when about to leave the rock, climbs on the back of its mother, and is by her carried down to the water. The Puffin, or Sea-parrot (*Fratercula arctica*) is a round, little, black-and-white bird, with a singular parrot-shaped beak, ribbed with orange. It frequents the same sort of places as the Guillemot, and its habits are similar, except that it does not expose its egg without protection. Where it finds holes, or crevices ready made to its use, it helps itself freely to them, and will even disperse rabbits, driving them out of their burrows. But when no holes are to be found, the male-bird makes a burrow to the depth of three or four feet, digging out the ground with his strong bill. In this burrow is laid the solitary egg, which is hatched after a month's incubation.

* *Vide* Waterton.

Of the Pelican family (*Pelicanidæ*) there are three British species, the Cormorant, the Shag, and the Gannet. These are birds of much more active habits than the last-named family, with bodies of more shapely form, more ample wings, and stronger flight. Their most remarkable characteristic is a surface of naked skin about the throat, capable of considerable dilatation, so as to serve as a pouch for conveying unswallowed food. This skin in the true Pelican is developed into an enormous bag. In its British representatives it is comparatively but rudimentary. The Cormorant (*Phalacrocorax carbo*) is a dusky bird, with blackish body, lighter-coloured wings, a crested pole, a yellow face, a long, slender-hooked bill, and green eyes. It may be seen on most parts of the coast perched on rocks, or sitting on the ledges of mural cliffs, watching for fish. Occasionally, in winter, it flies inland, and pursues its game in rivers and lakes; but its usual haunt is the rocky shore. It is a most expert fish-catcher, and formerly in this country was domesticated, and employed in taking fish for its master. Old writers give many accounts of this practice. In China, to the present day, an allied species (*Ph. sinensis*) is employed for the same purpose. I copy the account given by a recent traveller in that country. "There were two small boats, containing one man and about ten or twelve birds in each. The birds were standing perched on the sides of the little boat, and apparently had just arrived at the fishing-ground. They were now ordered out of the boat by their masters; and so well trained were they that they went on the water immediately, scattered themselves over the canal, and began to look for fish. They have a beautiful sea-green eye, and, quick as lightning, they see and dive upon the finny tribe, which, once caught in the sharp-notched bill of the bird, never, by any possibility, can escape. The Cormorant now rises to the surface, with the fish in his bill, and the moment he is seen by the Chinaman he is called back to the boat. As docile as a dog, he swims after his master, and allows himself to be pulled into the san-pan, where he disgorges his prey, and again resumes his labours. And, what is more wonderful still, if one of the Cormorants gets hold of a fish of large size, so large that he would have some difficulty in taking it to the boat, some of the others, seeing his dilemma, hasten to his assistance, and with their efforts united capture the animal, and haul him off to the boat. Sometimes a bird seemed to get lazy or playful, and swam about without attending to his business; and then the Chinaman, with a long bamboo, which he also used for propelling the boat, struck the water near where the bird was, calling out to him in an angry tone. Immediately, like the truant schoolboy, who neglects his lessons and is found out, the Cormorant gives up his play, and resumes his labours. A small string is put round the neck of the bird, to prevent him from swallowing the fish which he catches."[*] The Shag (*Ph. graculus*) is very similar in aspect and habits to the Common Cormorant, but is of smaller size, and is at once distinguished by its uniform dark-green colour. The Gannet (*Sula alba*) is more robust than either of the Cormorants, with a shorter and thicker neck, a large head, and a broadly conical,

---

[*] Fortune's China, pp. 99, 100.

very sharp and strong bill. The prevalent colour of the full-plumaged bird is white, the tips of its wings only being black, and some black lines about the face, resembling eyebrows or spectacles. The naked skin of the face is blue, the eyes pale yellow, and the head and neck buff-colour. The plumage of the young bird is very different, being blackish, spotted irregularly with small white specks. The habits of the Gannet are strictly marine, and it breeds, like other sea-birds, on precipitous rocks, where it forms a rude nest of reeds and grass. In some localities, as on the island-rock of St. Kilda, and others of the Hebrides, the Gannets congregate in vast numbers. Twenty-two thousand birds, besides immense numbers of eggs, are annually consumed in St. Kilda alone, without seriously injuring the colony. The birds are still so numerous there that it is supposed they destroy annually a hundred millions of herrings. Their mode of fishing is quite peculiar, and singularly graceful. Hovering to and fro, with rapid flight, over the surface of the sea, when it spies a fish swimming below, the Gannet suddenly rises perpendicularly over the spot, and then, closing its wings, drops head foremost on its prey, with more than arrowy speed, and almost unerring aim. It feeds entirely on fish, and chiefly on the various kinds of herrings. Besides those captured for food, large numbers are annually destroyed for the sake of the valuable down.

The family of *Laridæ*, containing the Gulls, Terns, and Petrels, has been incidentally mentioned in a former chapter. It consists of a large number of species peculiarly oceanic in their habits, and widely scattered over the world. Many of the species, besides visiting the shores of Northern Europe and Arctic America, extend their flights to far southern latitudes, and some appear to live constantly on the open sea, except when they visit the shore in the breeding-season. All are remarkable for the strength of their flight, and the easy grace of their motions as they soar or glide through the air with a scarcely perceptible movement of wing; but some are much more active than others. Their form is elegant and well-proportioned : some, as the Terns, resemble Swallows in shape and rapidity of flight; and others, as several of the gulls, seem analogous to pigeons. Almost all undergo remarkable changes of plumage at different ages, and some have also an annual change, the colours at the breeding-season becoming darker. This change rapidly takes place, without any moulting, the feathers of the head, which are originally white, gradually assuming a dark-brown or black colour. These birds are mostly voracious feeders, seizing indifferently on dead or living animal substances found floating on the sea, or thrown up at the recess of the tide. Large flocks both of Gulls and Terns are then busy with the Mollusca and Radiata on the sands; and at other times they may be seen hovering over the water, on the watch for any floating animal substance. This they perceive from a considerable height, and secure by a rapid descent and pounce; sometimes by merely curving down and skimming the surface; at other times, by closing the wings, and dropping suddenly under water. Both sexes in the gulls have similar plumage; but the males are known by being of larger size than the female. Their cry is

THE KITTY-WAKE AND SKUA.

peculiar, between a scream and a laugh, and, if heard in their wilder haunts, among precipitous rocks, and dashing waves, however discordant, is not unpleasing, when, perhaps, it is the only sound proceeding from a living thing that disturbs the solitude. Heard, as I have often heard it, on the summit of cliffs eight or nine hundred feet high, rising from the depths below, where each individual bird looks like a floating speck of foam, it gives a spirit to the scene that ever after attaches to the recollection of it. Various are the species of Gulls that breed upon our coasts, and various the stations they prefer. The Kitty-wake (*Larus tridactylus*), so called from its cry, prefers the highest and steepest crags, where it perches its sea-weed nest on almost inaccessible ledges. Others build on flatter shores, or less secluded places. Some, like the Skua (*Lestris cataractes*), have been called parasites, from their predaceous habits. "They rarely take the trouble to fish for themselves; but, watching the Gulls while thus employed, they no sooner observe one to have been successful than they immediately give chase, pursuing it with fury, and obliging it, from fright, to disgorge the recently-swallowed fish; they descend after it to catch it, and are frequently so rapid and certain in their movements and aim, as to seize their prize before it reaches the water."* From the nature of their food all the birds of the family are extremely oily, and many have the habit, when captured, of vomiting up quantities of clear oil, of a very offensive smell, and this apparently as a means of defence. The Fulmar (*Procellaria glacialis*), a large grey

* Yarrell, vol. iii. p. 603.

and white species, that forms very populous colonies on some of the remoter western islands of Scotland, and is occasionally seen elsewhere, is remarkable for the quantity of this oil which it disgorges. Yet, notwithstanding its strong-tasted flesh, it is eagerly sought after by the islanders, who annually consume many thousands of the young birds, besides multitudes of eggs. In pursuit of these the intrepid fowler has to ascend or descend frightful precipices, or to hang suspended in mid-air. The birds, according to Mr. Macgillivray, build only on the steep faces of the cliff, where small patches of grass here and there occur: " The nest is formed of herbage, seldom bulky, generally a mere shallow excavation in the turf, lined with dried grass and the withered tufts of sea-pink, in which the bird deposits a single egg, of a pure white colour when clean, which is seldom the case, and varying in size from two and a half to three inches in length, by two inches in breadth." The smallest bird of the family, and the smallest web-footed bird known, is the Storm Petrel (*Thalassidroma pelagica*), well known to mariners by the name of Mother Carey's Chicken, and dreaded by them from its supposed appearance immediately before a storm. In a sailor's superstition it is believed to rise out of the sea. This little creature lives almost constantly at sea, except during the breeding-season, when it visits maritime rocks, and unfrequented parts of the coast, and there deposits its solitary egg in holes or crevices. It feeds on any floating animal substance, or on such small soft animals as it can master; and when at sea, may be seen constantly flying about hither and thither, at a short distance from the surface, on the watch for prey. Its name, Petrel, is given, Mr. Yarrell tells us, from its "habit of paddling along the surface, from the Apostle Peter, who walked on the sea."

STORM PETREL.

The last little bird of which we have spoken ends the list of our marine birds, and naturally suggests to us a storm, as a storm does a shipwreck; and from a shipwreck to floating pieces of timber, or drift-wood, the passage is easy and natural. We shall now inquire whether such floating spars are worth examining. They often come ashore covered externally with Barnacles, and pierced through and through by the *Teredo* and *Limnoria*. All these animals have something interesting in their history. The Common Barnacle

(*Pentelasmis anatifera*) has a fabulous history sufficiently amusing, indicated by the specific name, *anatifera*. Our ancestors believed that Barnacle-geese were the offspring of these marine creatures: and worthy Master Gerard gives a circumstantial account of the whole process, and moreover prefaces it with a voucher, that tellers of marvellous tales are apt freely to offer,— "What our eyes have seen, and hands have touched, we shall declare." Nor is this all, for he favours us with a figure representing the metamorphosis going on. The Barnacle belongs to a very curious class of animals, called *Cirrhipoda*, which combine the characters of Crustacea and Mollusca in a remarkable manner, and, though usually placed with the latter, are, perhaps, nearer akin to the former. The Barnacle is lodged within a white shell, flattened at the sides, opening by a slit down one edge, and fixed on a soft, flexible, fleshy stalk. The shell is composed of five pieces, joined together by membranes. Within this coat of mail lies the soft body of the Barnacle, with its head towards the lower end of the

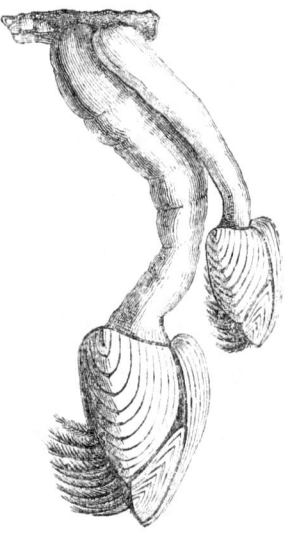

PENTELASMIS ANATIFERA.

shell, near the place where it is fixed to the stalk, and its tail at the upper extremity. The tail is not unlike that of a Crustacean, and is bordered on each side with six lobes (representing the segments of the articulate body of that class), each of which supports a pair of long, ciliated arms, or *cirrhi*, the whole resembling a plume of purple feathers. These cirrhi, when the animal is alive, are constantly in motion, projecting outward, and expanding into an oval, concave net, then retracting inwards, and closing upon whatever may have come within their reach. They are so placed that any small matter which becomes entangled within them can rarely escape, and finds a ready passage to the mouth. Very similar to the Barnacle is the animal of the *Balanus*, whose shells cover, in scurfy patches, the surface of exposed rocks, as well as drift-wood, or any other submerged substance. These shells are usually white, shaped like truncated cones, and composed of several ribbed pieces closely fitted together, with an aperture at top, closed by an operculum, and within this house the creature is lodged. Like the Barnacle, it puts out its arms in search of food, though to a less extent. There are many varieties of both kinds; that is to say, of the sessile and stalked Cirrhipoda. Some of the former, of large size, form a lodgment in the coats of Whales; others lodge themselves in Corals or Sponges. The habits of the race are very uniform. Once fixed, they remain so during their lives, taking chance for subsistence. In an early stage, however, they are free to move from place to place, and are lively little beings, swimming about with the speed of Water-fleas (*Daphniæ*), which active animals they resemble in many points. This affords another link by which the Cirrhipoda are connected with Crustacea. The young Cirrhipode bears little or no resemblance to its mature condition. It is about the tenth of an inch long, lodged in a pair of shelly valves, united like those of a bivalve shell, and large enough to admit of the whole animal being withdrawn into them. This shell opens in front, to allow the animal to extend its legs and arms. It has two long arms, furnished with a sucker and hooks, and six pairs of legs, formed for swimming. These are so arranged as to act in concert, and by their simultaneous stroke on the water to drive the little body forward in a succession of bounds. It has also a tail, tipped with four bristles, and commonly folded up under the body; and it has a pair of large pedunculated eyes. The whole animal is so like one of the humbler Crustaceans, that it might well pass for one of them.

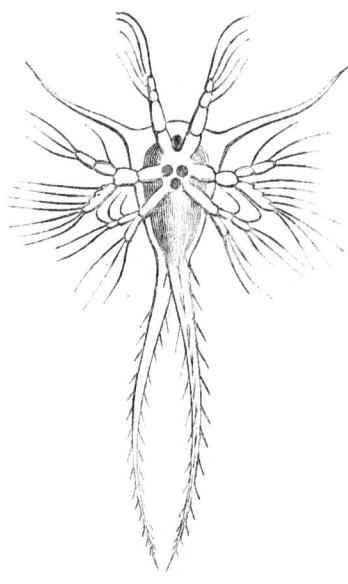

YOUNG CIRRHIPODE, MAGNIFIED.

But the acute observer (Mr. J. V. Thompson) who first discovered it, had the satisfaction of watching its change from this active life to the sedentary state of a Balanus. The animal fixes itself, the shell is gradually formed, ciliated arms or cirrhi take the place of feet, and the eyes are cast away, as being no longer needed. Here we have another instance of what looks like a retrograde developement; but this apparent anomaly is to conduct us to a division of the animal kingdom in which the external organs are less perfect than in the groups below them, but the internal organization, and especially the nervous system, is more complete.

Barnacles attach themselves to the surface of ships' timbers, and their pendant bodies, if suffered to remain, will materially obstruct the ship's motion or way. But they do no further damage. There are, however, other Mollusca, the *Teredines*, or Ship-worms, whose attacks are far more fatal. These are not contented with a superficial station, but seek a secure resting-place within the log; and, when once they take up their residence, soon riddle the substance through and through, reducing the wood to a mere shell. Any wood-work constantly submerged is subject to their attacks, and it is astonishing with what rapidity the work of destruction goes on. Piles of solid pine-timber, of large size, have been proved to be perfectly destroyed within five years. The *Teredo* enters at any part of the surface, but soon bends its course in the direction of the grain, and forms a burrow some feet in length, and varying from a quarter to half an inch in diameter. This he lines, as he proceeds, with a shelly coat secreted by his mantle, but without any attachment to his person. It is merely a sort of plaster to the walls of his singular house. He himself dwells at the far end of the chamber, enclosed in a bivalve shell resembling that of a *Pholas*. The long worm-like body which fills the burrow is merely the extension of the siphonal tubes, which in this genus are of great length. The organization of the body is not very unlike that of other CONCHIFERA,* and fluid enters and is expelled through the siphons in a similar way. By the older writers the *Teredo* was placed among the Annelides, near *Serpula;* but this false position was corrected as soon as the nature of the animal was understood : in modern works we find it associated with *Pholas*, to which its organization and habits closely ally it. Its ravages have caused it to be observed from very early times, and many large books have been devoted to its history. Formerly, before the practice of coppering ships became general, many a stately vessel fell a sacrifice to its prowess ; and about the middle of the last century fears were entertained for the safety of Holland, the *Teredo* having attacked the piles on which that singular country rests. Thus navies can with difficulty resist the attacks of a little creature apparently so unimportant ; and a country that braved the power of Spain in her days of strength, was well-nigh sinking under the gnawing of a worm. On our own coast similar destruction is going on in many places. No less than six species are included in the British list of *Teredines ;* but the most undoubted

* See p. 34.

CHELURA AND LIMNORIA.

native of our shores is what is now called *T. norvagicus*, the *T. navalis* of most British writers, though not of Linnæus. This species is of large size, and as active in mischief as the true *navalis*. Mr. Thompson gives an interesting account of the rapidity with which it has destroyed wood-work in the harbour of Port Patrick; and, according to Mrs. Griffiths, the same species caused the destruction of the bridge at Teignmouth. It has been observed on various other parts of our coast, engaged in its constant task,—reducing beams of timber to dust, and undoing with persevering industry what the "lord of the creation" is at most pains to do.

CHELURA AND LIMNORIA.

In this task of undoing, the *Teredo* does not work alone. The wood-work that escapes his auger may fall to powder under the teeth of two minute Crustaceous animals (*Limnoria terebrans* and *Chelura terebrans*), not so big as a grain of rice, but as active as "the mother of mischief" herself, and as untiring. These little creatures, which resemble minute Wood-lice, or Shrimps, attack, like the *Teredo*, any submerged wood-work, and rapidly perforate it in all directions, till it is reduced to a mere shell, ready to fall to pieces on the slightest touch. The *Limnoria*, which is the larger of the two, bores directly into the timber, piercing deeply nearly at right angles with the surface; while the *Chelura* excavates obliquely, rather ploughing up the surface than forming a deep burrow. Its work of destruction proceeds with fearful rapidity, particularly where it follows, as is often the case, its friend, the *Limnoria*. The loosened surface is rapidly washed away by the action of the water, and a new one exposed, to be in turn ploughed over by the busy creature. Though the means in action seem small, if we regard merely the size of these destructive insects, yet, when countless multitudes establish themselves in a beam, the untiring play of their jaws soon reduces the most solid timber to powder. Nor is it only constantly submerged timber which suffers from them. They can endure to be left dry at low-water, and the *Limnoria* has been kept alive for a considerable time in its burrow by merely an occasional moistening of salt and water.*

Among the objects which occasionally float ashore, or drift about with the waves, are dark-coloured, roundish, or spindle-shaped bodies, of the size and colour of grapes,

* Kirby and Spence, vol. i. p. 204 in note (6th edit.) An excellent account of the *Limnoria* has been published by Dr. Coldstream, in Brewster's Journal; and Professor Allman has given us a most elaborate paper on *Chelura*, in which the structure of the animal is very fully detailed, in the Annals of Natural History, vol. xix. p. 361.

MARINE GRAPES. 239

and hanging together in clusters. They are soft to the touch, with a tough skin, resembling Indian-rubber; one end is produced into a sort of point or nipple, and the other fixed to a fleshy stalk, which coils round seaweed, or other floating objects, and serves to fix the berry-like bag in its place. These bags, are the eggs of Cuttle-fish. At an early stage they contain a white yolk, enclosed in a clear albumen; and nearer maturity, the young Cuttle-fish may be found within, in various stages of formation. At last, when fully formed, the leathery bag is rent asunder, and the young Cuttle-fish enters on his career. Cuttle-fishes are, perhaps, the most singular in structure of all the marine animals we commonly meet with, and are interesting to

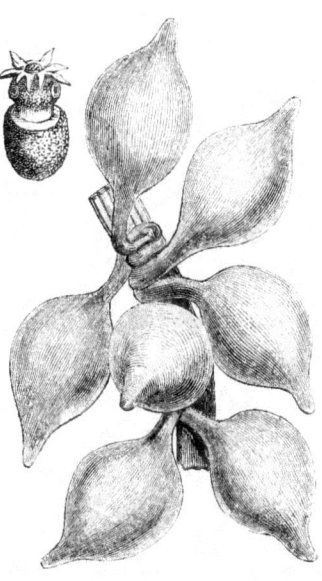

MARINE GRAPES.

the naturalist in a variety of ways. If it were only for the position which they occupy in our systematic arrangements, at the head of the great group of the Mollusca, and in close proximity to the Vertebrates, their history would be important, from its exhibiting points of union between these subdivisions of the animal kingdom. In fact while all their salient characters are those of Molluscous animals, and some of them are furnished with shells formed like those of other Mollusca, there are evident traces of an internal skeleton, which, in the manner in which it is evolved and nourished, is exactly analogous to the skeleton of a Vertebrate, in what may be supposed its most rudimentary form. The principal mass of nervous matter, or, as we may call it, the brain, is lodged in an obvious skull : the eyes are of a type of structure much more perfect than in any other Mollusc, and approaching closely to the complex structure of this organ in Vertebrates ; it has a set of olfactory nerves, and a well-formed ear ; and the nerve of taste is well developed, if we may judge by the vascular character and mobility of the tongue. In all that constitutes the life of the animal, in his internal organs, his senses, and his intelligence, the Cuttle-fish, therefore, approaches very closely to a Vertebrate. Yet this creature has a body unlike anything we are accustomed to meet with among the higher animals, and whose similitude we must seek at the very base of the animal kingdom, among the Polypes themselves. In those lowly-organized creatures we found a bag-like body, with a mouth at one end, surrounded by a number of long arms, or tentacles, spreading round it in the form of a star. Here we again meet with the same type, or general idea, but in a state of advancement perhaps the greatest that such a type of organization admits of : instead of being minute gelatinous

CUTTLE-FISHES.

creatures, such as the *Hydra* of our ponds, some of the animals of which we now speak, if travellers' stories may be trusted, more nearly resemble in their size, terrific aspect, and destructive powers, the Hydra of fabulous history. On our own shores there are many species, not, however, of a formidable size; but in tropical countries, species are said to occur with arms "nine fathoms long,"* which do not scruple to attack man himself, and to do so not merely when he is found naked in the water, but often when passing in a boat, which they sink with ease, by throwing their arms across it. Once the Cuttle-fish fixes his hold, no effort that a fish is capable of making can throw him off; and the peculiar arrangement of the limbs, added to their admirable structure, place the unfortunate prey at the mercy of a singularly hard and sharp pair of jaws, When the Cuttle-fish is at rest, he stands (like an *Echinus*) on his head, with his mouth in contact with the surface of what he stands upon; and round the mouth extends a circle of eight or ten arms, the whole of whose lower surface is studded with circular discs, of most elaborate structure, like so many cupping-glasses, or rather miniature air-pumps. When the Cuttle-fish wishes to fix himself to any surface, he merely brings these discs in contact with it, and then, exercising

* "A friend of mine, long resident among the Indian isles, and a diligent observer of Nature, informed me that the natives affirm, that some have been seen two fathoms broad over their centre, and each arm nine fathoms long. When the Indians navigate their little boats, they go in dread of them; and lest these animals should fling their arms over, and sink them, they never sail without an axe to cut them off."—Pennant, Brit. Zool. vol. iv. p. 45.

voluntary muscles, he creates a vacuum under each disc, and rests secure. If fixed on the back of a fish, the mandibles are now brought into direct contact with the prey, and rapidly devour it. It is in vain for the tortured victim to fly through the water; he carries his enemy with him, till he sinks exhausted under its fangs. In our Common Cuttle-fishes the suckers, or discs, hold their prey simply by the power of suction; but there are species in which this fearful prehensile apparatus is rendered still more perfect by a sharp hook fixed in the centre of every sucker. These are probably intended to retain soft and slippery prey, which might escape from suckers of an ordinary kind. While thus formidable to other animals, and amply provided with offensive weapons, we hardly expect to find weapons of a defensive character, such as the weakest animals depend upon. Yet we must remember that the body of the Cuttle-fish is soft and naked; that, though well-armed in front, it may readily be attacked in the rear; and that, unless when able to attach itself by the discs of its arms, it is powerless to annoy. To escape, therefore, when surprised, it resorts to stratagem. Nature has furnished it with an internal bag, that secretes a large quantity of a deep-brown fluid, which, on the approach of danger, it can squirt out with force in the face of its foe, and which, mixing readily with the water, forms round the Cuttle-fish an opaque cloud, that puzzles his pursuer, and favours his escape. This inky fluid, thus useful to its owner, is often the cause of his destruction by man, who applies it to his own purposes. It is from this substance that the pigment called *sepia*, so invaluable to painters in water-colours, is prepared. And it is a curious fact (tested by Dr. Buckland) that the contents of the ink-bag of fossil species retain all the chromatic property, and have been used with success in the arts. The sepia commonly in use is prepared from an Indian species; but the Cuttle-fishes of our own shores yield an equally valuable dye.

No British Cuttle-fish possesses an external shell, though furnished with an internal one, in the shape of a horny or calcareous, lanceolate, or somewhat boat-shaped body, lodged in a cavity of the mantle; exactly analogous to the shelly plates of such Mollusca as *Aplysia* and *Limax*. But one of the most beautiful of all shells —the Argonaut, or Paper Nautilus—is the coat of an animal of this class, not very unlike a common Cuttle-fish in form, and having an organization essentially similar. Alas for poetry!—the stories of the Argonaut, believed for nearly two thousand years, are now exploded. Modern observers have clearly shown that the Argonaut does not make use of its expanded arms as sails, or its tapering legs as oars, or of its keeled shell as a boat; but, on the contrary, that it passes most of its time crawling on the bottom of the sea, like a snail, with its shell turned keel upwards; and that when it does swim through the water, as it can do with great speed, its arms and legs are applied to purposes very different from oars or sails. The arms (*sails*) are closely pressed to the surface of the shell, which they cover completely with a fleshy coat; and the taper legs (*oars*) are brought together, and directed in a straight line from the head. And thus prepared for swimming, the

Argonaut drives itself backwards at a rapid rate, by alternate imbibition and expulsion of water through its siphon. The Pearly or Chambered Nautilus is the shell of another animal of this class, considerably different in organization from the Cuttle-fish or the Argonaut, and obviously of a lower type of structure. It essentially differs from either in having *four*, instead of *two*, sets of gills, and has therefore been placed by Professor Owen in a distinct order, of which it forms almost the only living representative. Very different, however, was the condition of this order in the waters of the early world, where species of Nautilus and of allied forms existed in great profusion. Upwards of sixty fossil species of Nautilus are found in British strata, with many hundred kinds of Ammonites, Orthoceratites, &c., genera which are no longer known to exist in a living state. And it is exceedingly remarkable that our modern Nautilus belongs to a generic type which has existed from the earliest times, from which remains of animals of this class have been preserved; while many extensive genera of similar animals of later creation have become totally extinct. Thus, of the true Ammonites, or Snake-stones, —fossils resembling the horns of Jupiter Ammon, and which were inhabited by animals resembling the animal of the Nautilus,—though many hundreds flourished in times long posterior to the creation of Nautili, and none were in existence so early as the first true Nautilus, not one has come down living to the modern sea, and the last members of the race were entombed in the chalk deposits. The successive changes which have passed over the animal and vegetable worlds in revolving ages offer us subjects of contemplation of the most interesting character, in which the mind is at one time carried back to what has been " before the world was," and at others, stretches equally forward to what shall be hereafter. In tracing fossil remains in strata, deposited at successive periods, we come to beds in which remarkable forms, such as the Ammonite, meet us for the first time ; and, having ascertained that none exist in any *lower* bed, we are forced to admit that, at the time when that bed was in course of formation these creatures were first introduced on the stage of life. All *lower* beds tell of a creation existing *before* them, and the animals contained in such are therefore older denizens of the world. Again, having fixed the stratum in which the Ammonite first appears, we examine the strata above it, and find the number of those fossils gradually increasing, until we reach a bed in which the genus attains its maximum;— and thence we find a gradual diminution of species in all superior beds. No new forms are introduced, but the old ones drop off one by one, until at last the whole race disappears—every species of the extensive group being numbered with the dead. Nor is this a solitary instance of what researches into the fossil world reveal to us. It is the general lot of every organic being introduced into the world. Not only are the individual animals mortal, but the very species are destined to destruction. Some types have a longer life than others. The Nautilus still maintains its ground, though its genus dates back untold ages before the creation of the Ammonite, whose last representative must have perished ages before the creation of man. We see the whole life of the Ammonite genus—and we can perceive, by its diminished number, that the Nautilus is approaching its close. But the circumstances which regulate the extinction of the one or the other are unknown to us. Changes of climate may now and then cause the destruction of a race; but the extinction of species, and of generic types, seems to proceed on too regular a plan to be dependent on secondary causes, and must, I think, be referred to laws originally imposed on each species at its creation.

What those laws are, we can but conjecture. All analogy favours the notion that creation has been progressive; for everything about us tells of a beginning, an upward progress, and a decline. And the history of the earth, so far as we can decipher the hieroglyphics written in its strata, furnishes evidence of such progress. Doubtless there was a time when "the world was without form and void, and darkness was upon the face of the deep," and doubtless the altered aspect of all things springs from that Power which "moved upon the face of the waters," and called forth light, and life, and order, out of chaos. Ages rolled on, and new animals and plants were introduced, each, as it successively appeared, a witness to the power, and wisdom, and personality of its Author. To His personality clearly. For though we may admit that physical laws suffice to explain the mutations of the mineral world,—the regular succession of seasons, and the irregular action of the earthquake and he storm, we cannot attribute to physical agency the existence of organic life—itself the clearest witness to a supernatural power. Every plant and every animal is, while its life endures, a personal fellow-worker with the Deity, — not creating as He creates, absolutely, but an author of relative creations —an agent in His hand of changes which force merely physical could never compass. The growth of cellular or vascular tissue, whereby the body, once but a living speck, becomes what God has destined it to become;— the internal action of organized bodies;—animal will; —the reproduction of the species;—all these are utterly antagonistic to the physical laws of matter. They are manifestations of that other agency—Life, an attribute of the personal God:—and while the portion of life committed to each lasts, the body performs its wondrous functions. To life it owed its power of growth, and when life is taken from it the laws of matter resume their sway, and the organized body gradually returns to its mineral condition. Take the lime, the phosphorus, the sulphur, the carbon, and the other mineral and gaseous substances, of which the human frame consists. Chemistry demonstrates to us that of such and such quantities of each of these a human body is composed. She can decompose any organic frame into similar elements, but what power can build it up again from the dust? Who can make the "dry bones live?" Organic life is therefore a witness to the power which works by it, and that power is God. And organic life has been progressive. In its earlier days the world was unfit for the dwelling of man—how much unfit we cannot tell; and it was tenanted by a Fauna and Flora wholly different from that which the naturalist now sees about him. Gradually the elder races died out and were succeeded by new types, each successively more and more like the present creation. Gradually, we may suppose, the earth and air became more like their present condition. At length "in the fulness of time" man was introduced, destined to become the lord of this present creation, and finally, the inheritor of a better world. Whether man's race, like that of every other animated being, be doomed to come to a close, it is not the province of natural history to inquire; but it seems to me that no one who accepts as truth the doctrine of the Incarnation,—and considers what that stupendous miracle involves,—can look forward, as some speculative minds have done, to any further developement of the animal creation. Here, then, the naturalist reaches his proper limits—the horizon that bounds his powers of vision :—if he would still look further, and learn more of his relation to his Maker, he must carry his researches into other fields, and seek for

—— Blumen und Früchte,
Gereift auf einer andern Flur,
In einem andern Sonnenlichte,
In einer glücklichern Natur.
Schiller.

INDEX AND GLOSSARY.

A.

Abranchiate (*Annelides*), 126.
Acalephæ (Jelly Fishes), 183; structure, 186; classification, 186; *Pulmonigrade* order, 187; *Ciliograde*, 188; *Physograde*, 189; *Cirrhigrade*, 190; reproduction and metamorphosis, 192-198.
Acephala, testaceous, (*Conchifera,* or *Bivalve Mollusca,*) 34; structure of animal, 35; habits, 37, 38; food, 39; structure of shells, 39, 40; classification, 40.
Acephala, tunicated, (see *Mollusca tunicata*).
Acetabularia (a Mediterranean sea plant), 62.
Actinia mesembryanthemum (Common Sea Anemone), 50.
Actiniæ (Sea Anemonies), described, 91; their structure, 92.
Adductor muscles, of a bivalve mollusc, are those which hold the valves of the shell together, see page 36.
Agar-Agar (an East Indian seaweed), 75.
Albatross, 24.
Alcadæ (a family of sea-birds), 222, 223.
Alcyonium digitatum (Dead-men's Toes; one of the Zoophytes of the order *Asteroida*), account of, 47, 48; alluded to, 151.

Alga, pl. *Algæ* (Sea-weeds). A large class of Cryptogamic plants inhabiting salt and fresh water. An outline of their history will be found in Chapter III., and an account of some microscopic kinds (*Diatomaceæ*) in Chapter VI. page 170, &c.
Algologist: one who investigates the history of the *Algæ* or Seaweeds.
Alva marina (*Zostera*), used for bedding, 49.
Ambulacra: spaces on the shell or skin of an Urchin or Star-fish, pierced with rows of holes, through which sucking-feet are protruded, 42, 137.
Ammophila arundinacea (Sandreed), 12.
Amphidotus cordatus (Heart Urchin), described, 41.
Amphitrite (one of the *Annelides*), 130.
Analogue, ⎫ When two plants or
Analogous, ⎬ animals of different
Analogy. ⎭ orders or genera resemble each other in habit, or in some prominent character, and appear to occupy a similar position in the groups to which they respectively belong, such plants or animals are said to be *analogues* one of another.
Anatidæ (an order of Sea-birds, containing Ducks and Geese), 218.

INDEX AND GLOSSARY.

Annelides (Red-blooded Worms) described, 125; classification, 126; *Abranchiata*, 126; *Dorsibranchiata*, 127; *Tubicola*, 127; various examples, 128–131.
Anthozoa (a sub-class of Zoophytes), 86; division into orders, 86; examples, 87–94.
Aplysia (a Sea-Slug), 108.
Aphrodite aculeata (Sea Mouse) described, 132.
Arca (a genus of shells), 40.
Arenaria rubra, 210.
Arenicola piscatorum (Lug Worm), 127.
Argonaut, 243.
Armeria (Sea Pink), 207.
Ascidiæ (Sea Squirts), their history, 97, 98; compound, 98.
Asperula cynandrica, 211.
Aster tripolium, 207.
Asteriadæ (a family of Star-fishes), 137; examples of, 138–141.
Asteroida (an order of Zoophytes), 86; described, 150; British species of, 151–153.

B.

Bacillaria paradoxa (a minute *Alga*), motion of, 177.
Balani, 50, 233.
Barnacle (*Pentelasmis anatifera*) 229.
Beroe, 188.
Beta maritima (Wild Beet), 209.
Bird-cities, 223.
Bird's-head appendage of *Cellulariæ*, 97.
Bivalve Mollusca (*Acephala*), 34, &c.; classification, 40.
Bostrychia scorpioides, 209.
Botany, pleasures of, 13.
Botryllidæ (a family of compound *Ascidians*), 99.

Branchiæ, } The gills, or
Branchial-fringe, } breathing apparatus of submerged animals.
Bryozoa (or *Polyzoa*, a sub-class of Zoophytes), 86, 95; examples, 96; affinity with *Ascidiæ*, 97.
Bryopsis plumosa, 61.
Buccinum undatum, 32; its proboscis, 110.

C.

Cabbage, wild, 206.
Callithamnion (a genus of seaweed), 72.
Carapace, the principal body-shell of a Crab or Lobster, 156.
Cardium (Cockle), 40.
Caryophyllea Smithii, 93.
Chelura terebrans, its destructive habits, 237.
Chione, 39.
Chiton, 109.
Chlorospermeæ (the green *Algæ*), 56; structure, 57; distribution, 59; examples, 56–62.
Chondrus crispus (Carrigeen), 73, 74.
Chough (Red-legged Crow), 217.
Cilia, minute vibratory hairs found on various parts, external or internal, of the bodies of the lower animals,
Ciliograde, Jelly-fishes, 188.
Cirrhigrade, Jelly-fishes, 190.
Cirrhipoda, a class of animals combining the characters of *Mollusca* and *Crustacea*, described, 232; examples and history, 232–235.
Cladophora, 57, 62.
Climate, influence on vegetation, 66.
Cochlearia (Scurvy-grass), 207.
Cockle, its animal, 36.
Codium tomentosum, 60.
Colymbidæ (a family of sea-birds), 221.

Colymbus glacialis (Northern Diver), 222.
Comatula (Feather Star), 134, 135.
Conchifera (see *Acephala*), 34.
Conchology, importance of, 101.
Convolvulus Soldanella, 213.
Convolvuli (Persian), 213.
Coral-banks, 46.
Corals, 84.
Corallineæ (an order of sea-weeds), 75.
Cormorant fishing in China, 225.
Coryne pusilla, 87.
Crab, young of, 165; various kinds of Crabs described, 161-164.
Cray-fish, change of shell, 157.
Cruciferous plants, 206.
Crustacea (a class of articulated animals) described, 154; affinity with insects, 154; their gills, 155; change of shell, 155; voluntary dismemberment, 158; varieties of form, 159; organs of locomotion, 160, 161; examples, 160, &c.
Cuttle-fish, eggs, 239; structure and history, 239-241; *Sepia*, 242; fossil, 243.
Cyclobranchiata (an order of Gasteropodous *Mollusca*), 109.
Cypræa, 112.

D.

Dead-men's Toes (*Alcyonium*), 47.
Delesseria, 72.
Desmidieæ, 171; Mr. Ralfs on, 171.
Diatomaceæ, 171-176.
Dog-fish egg (Mermaid's-purse), 31.
Dorsibranchiate Annelides, 127; variety and beauty of, 131.
Drag, 119.
Dredge, Naturalist's, 117.
Drift-wood, 230.
Dunlin (*Tringa variabilis*), 23.

E.

Echinidæ (Sea Urchins), 43; affinities and fossil species, 42, 43.
Echinus Sphæra (Egg Urchin), description and history, 143; structure of shell, 144; dental apparatus, 146-148.
Ectocarpus (a genus of sea-weed), 71.
Encrinitis (Lily Stones), 133.
Enteromorpha (a genus of sea-weed), 57.
Entomology, the history of insects, 16.
Epiphyte, a vegetable which attaches its roots to the surface of another vegetable, for the purpose of support, but does not draw nourishment from the stem it adheres to,
Eringium (Eringo), 206.
Escharidæ (a family of *Polyzoa*), 206.
Euphorbia paralias, 212; African species of *Euphorbia*, 212.
Euphrasia (Eye-bright), 211.

F.

Fanciful systems, 2.
Fauna, a name applied by Linnæus to a history of the animals of any particular district, as *Flora* is used for a local history of plants.
Feather Star (*Comatula*), 134, 135.
Florideæ (see *Rhodospermeæ*), a sub-class of sea-weeds.
Flustra foliacea, 44.
Foot-prints and marks on the sands, 25.
Foraminifera, minute shell-coated animals, 180; examples of, 180, 181; their affinities, 182.
Fratercula arctica (Puffin), 224.
Fregilus graculus (Chough), 217.

INDEX AND GLOSSARY.

Frustule, a term applied to the cells or articulations of the *Diatomaceæ*, &c., 172.
Fucus (a genus of sea-weed), 63; its common species, 63, 64; varieties of *F. vesiculosus*, 66.
Fulmar (*Procellaria glacialis*), 229.

G.

Gannet (*Sula alba*), 226.
Gasteropoda (a class of Molluscous animals) described, 105; structure of animal, 106; tongue, 106, 107; classification, 107; *Pulmonibranchiate* order, 107; *Nudibranchiate*, 108; *Tectibranchiate*, 108; *Pectinibranchiate*, 109; *Scutibranchiate*, 109; *Cyclobranchiate*, 109; habits and organisation, 110, 111.
Geology, pleasures of, 9.
Glauceum luteum (Horned Poppy), 206.
Glaux maritima, 209.
Goosander (*Mergus merganser*), 220.
Grasswrack (*Zostera*), 49.
Griffithsia corallina, 72.
Guillemot (*Uria troile*), 223.
Gulls, habits of, 227.

H.

Habitat, the place in which a plant or animal is found living.
Helichondria celata, 29.
Heart Urchins, 41.
Helianthemum (Rock-rose), 214, 215.
Helianthoida (an order of Zoophytes), 86, 91, 92.
Hermit-crab, (*Pagurus*), 112.
Holothuriadæ (Sea Cucumbers), 148; examples, 149; self-destructive habits, 150.

Horned Poppy (*Glaucium*), 206.
Hydroida (an order of Zoophytes), 86.

I. J.

Ianthina, (Blue Snail-shell), 192.
Ichthyology, the history of fishes, 16.
Iodine, 64.
Isthmia obliquata, 171.
Jelly-fishes (*Acalephæ*), 15; history of, 183; cause the phosphorescence of the sea, 184, 185. (See *Acalephæ*).

K.

Kelp, an impure carbonate of soda, obtained by burning *fuci*, 64.
Kitty-wake (*Larus tridactylus*), 229.

L.

Lagenæ, 180.
Laminaria, 53, 69.
Laridæ (a family of sea-birds, containing Gulls, &c.), 227.
Larus tridactylus (Kitty-wake), 229.
Lavatera arborea, 215.
Lepraliæ (minute Zoophytes), 96.
Lestris cataractes (Skua), 229.
Lichina (a genus of submarine Lichens), 68.
Licmophora flabellata, 172.
Ligament, a tough and elastic cartilage which connects the two valves of a bivalve shell, and serves as a hinge, 37.
Limnoria terebrans, destruction caused by, 237.
Limpet (*Patella*), 101; its tongue, 106.
Linnæus, 3.
Littorina littoralis, 25; degenerated variety of *L. rudis*, 103.

INDEX AND GLOSSARY.

Littoral zone, 56.
Lobster, its movements, 161.
Lucernaria, 94.
Lucina (a genus of shells), 41.
Lug Worm, 127.
Luidia (Lingthorn), its history, 139, 140.
Lutraria (a genus of shells), 40.

M.

Macrocystis, 69.
Mactra, 37. 40.
Madrepore coral, its formation, 92.
Madreporiform tubercle of Star-fishes, 141.
Maia squinado, 162.
Marine grapes, 239.
Masked Crab, 163.
Medusæ, 136.
Melanospermiæ (olive-coloured sea-weed), 56–63.
Melobesia lichenoides, 77; other kinds, 120.
Mergansers, 220; Red-breasted, 220.
Mergus albellus (Smew), 220; M. merganser (Goosander), 221.
Mermaid's Purse, 29.
Mesembryanthemum, a genus of plants with succulent leaves and starry flowers, often called Ficoides, 91.
Milkwort (Polygala), 211.
Mollusca—Mollusc and Molluscs (the name given to a large class of invertebrate animals, containing most shell-fish, slugs, &c.) described, 100; Testaceous Acephala, or Bivalve Mollusca, 34; Tunicated Mollusca, 97; Gasteropodous, 105.
Mother Cary's Chicken, 230.
Mussels, their habits, 105.
Mya (a genus of shells), 37.

N.

Nassa reticulata, 112.
Natica monilifera, 33.
Natatores (Swimmers, an order of birds), 217.
Nautilus, 243, 244; fossil species. 244.
Nereocystis (a great sea-weed), 69.
Northern Diver (Colymbus glacialis). 222.
Nudibranchiata (an order of Gasteropodous Mollusca), 108.
Nullipores, 120.

O.

Oarweed, root of, 53. 69.
Oidemia nigra (Scoter), 218.
Old oyster-shell, history of, 28.
Ophiocoma (a genus of Star-fishes), 136.
Ophiura (a genus of Star-fishes), 136.
Ophiuridæ (a family of Star-fishes) 136.
Orchis morio, 216.
Ornithology, the history of birds. 16.

P.

Padina Pavonia, 70.
Pagurus (Hermit-crab), 112.
Palmipes (Bird's-foot Sea-star), 139.
Parasite, a vegetable or animal which draws its nourishment from another.
Patella (Limpet), 101: P. pellucida and P. lævis, 120.
Pavonaria quadrangularis, 153.
Pecten (the Scallop), 39; animal of, 35.
Pectinibranchiata (an order of Gasteropodous Mollusca), 109.

254 INDEX AND GLOSSARY.

Pedicellaria, 143.
Pelicanidæ (a family of sea-birds), 225.
Pennatula phosphorea (Sea Pen), 151.
Pentelasmis (Barnacle), 231.
Perranzabuloe, 11.
Phalacrocorax (Cormorant), 225; fishing in China with *P. sinensis*, 225; *P. graculus* (Shag), 226.
Pholas, habits of, 104.
Phosphorescence of the sea, 185.
Physalia (Portuguese man-of-war), 189.
Physograde, Jelly-fishes, 189.
Pinnotheres (a small kind of Crab), 164.
Piran (St.), 10.
Planaria, 123-125.
Plantago, *P. maritima*, and *P. coronopus*, 203.
Plumularia cristata, 89.
Polygala (Milkwort), 211.
Polype, one of the individual animals of a Zoophyte.
Polypidom, the stony or horny skeleton of a Zoophyte.
Polysiphonia (a genus of sea-weed), 73, 74.
Pólyzoa, or *Bryozoa* (a class of Zoophytes with animals resembling *Ascidiæ*), 86, 95.
Porphyra laciniata, 58.
Portunidæ (Swimming Crabs), 162.
Procellaria glacialis (Fulmar), 229.
Pseudo, prefixed to words, signifies *false*.
Puffin, 224.
Pulmonibranchiata (an order of Gasteropodous Mollusca), 107.
Pulmonigrade, Jelly-fishes, 187.
Purpura lapillus, its eggs, 33.

R.

Ralfs, Mr. on Desmidieæ.
Razor-shell (*Solen*), 38.
Ray-fish, 29.
Red Sea, its colour, 178.
Rhodospermeæ (or *Florideæ*, the red coloured sea-weeds), 56-71.
Ripple-mark, 26.
Rissoa (a genus of shells), 122, 183.
Rosa spinosissima, 214.

S.

Sabella (one of the *Annelides*), 130.
Salicornia (jointed glass-wort) pickle made of, 208.
Salpa, history of, 199.
Samolus Valerandi, 210.
Sand-reed (*Ammophila*), 12.
Sands, wind-blown, 10; in Sligo, 11.
Sandy sea-shore, 21.
Scallop, animal of, 35.
Scilla verna and *autumnalis*, 215.
Scoter (*Oidemia nigra*), 218.
Scutibranchiata (an order of Gasteropodous Mollusca), 109.
Sea Anemone, 91, 92.
Sea-birds, 216.
Sea Cucumbers, 148.
Sea Lavender (*Statice*), 207.
Sea Mouse, 132.
Sea Pea, 13.
Sea Pen, 151.
Sea Pink (*Armeria*), 207.
Sea Slug, 108.
Sea Squirt, 97.
Sea Urchins, 97.
Sea-weeds, 13. 52-78.
Seaside plants, 205-216.
Season of rest, 67.
Sertularia, 87; *S. filicula*, 88; *S. operculata*, 89.

INDEX AND GLOSSARY.

Serpula, habits of, 128.
Shag (*Phalacrocorax graculus*), 226.
Shell-drake, 218.
Shelly-sand, 180.
Ship-worm, 235.
Silene maritima, 210.
Skate-barrows, 29.
Skua (*Lestris cataractes*), 229.
Smew (*Mergus albellus*), 220.
Solen (Razor-shell), 37, 38.
Spatangaceae, 43.
Species, decline of, 103; gradual extinction, 245-248.
Sphacelaria (a genus of sea-weed), 71.
Spider Crabs, 161.
Spiranthes autumnalis, 216.
Spondylus (a genus of shells), 39.
Sponges, their structure and variety, 81; eggs, 83.
Spores of *Algae*, 83.
Squills, 215.
Star-fishes, 42; history and classification, 132; skeleton, 138.
Statice (See Lavender), 207.
Storm Petrel, 230.
Sula alba (Gannet), 226.
Sun Star (*Solaster*), 138.
Swimming Crabs, 162.

T.

Tadorna vulpa (Shell-drake), 218.
Tamarix, 215.
Tectibranchiata (an order of Gasteropodous Mollusca), 108.
Tellina (a genus of shells), 39.
Tentacula, the soft arms or feelers of the lower animals, generally placed round the mouth : the *horns* of a snail, &c.
Terebella (one of the *Annelides*), 130.
Teredo (Ship-worm), 235.
Terns, or Sea Swallows, 24, 227.

Testacea, the Linnæan name for the shelly-coated Mollusca.
Thalassidroma pelagica (Storm Petrel, or Mother Cary's Chicken), 230.
Thrift (*Armeria*), 207.
Thyone papillosa, 149.
Tree, Mallow (*Lavatera*), 215.
Trichonema, 216.
Trifolium arvense, for winter nosegays, 212.
Tringa variabilis (Dunlin), 23.
Tubicola (an order of *Annelides*), 127.
Tubularia (a genus of Zoophytes), 87.
Turbinolia Milletiana, 93.

U.

Ulva latissima, 32.
Univalve Mollusca (*Gasteropoda*), 32, 105, &c.
Uria troile (Guillemot), 223.

V.

Vegetation of sandy downs, 211; salt marshes, 207; rocky soil, 214; grassy pastures, 215.
Velella (a genus of Jelly-fishes), 190.
Velvet Crab, 163.
Venus (a genus of shells), 37-39.
Viola tricolor (Wild Pansy), 211.
Virgularia mirabilis, 153.

W.

Water-fleas (*Dauphinæ*), 155.
White, Gilbert, his history of Selborne, 7.

X.

Xanthidia, fossil, 176.

Z.

Zoology, pleasures of, 14.
Zoophytes (a class of animals nearly the lowest in the scale of organisation, inhabiting the horny and stony corals. Individually these animals are called *polypes*, and their coral a *polypidom*), 44. 84, &c.
Zostera marina (Grass Wrack), 49.

LONDON:
Printed by S. & J. BENTLEY and HENRY FLEY.
Bangor House, Shoe Lane.

Milton Keynes UK
Ingram Content Group UK Ltd.
UKHW020623050324
438776UK00006B/1027